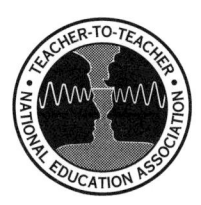

Teacher-to-Teacher Series

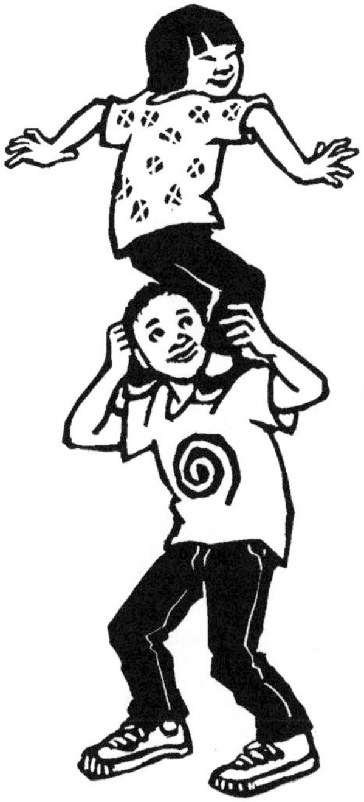

MULTI-AGE *classrooms*

NEA Teacher-to-Teacher Books

Copyright © 1995
National Education Association of the United States

Printing History
First Printing: July 1995

NOTE: The opinions expressed in this book should not be construed as representing the policy or position of the National Education Association. Materials published by the NEA Professional Library are intended to be discussion documents for educators who are concerned with specialized interests of the profession.

CREDITS: *Editor:* Karen Gutloff. *Production Coordinator:* Linda Brunson. *Art Design:* NoBul Graphics.

Library of Congress Cataloging-in-Publication Data
Multi-age Classrooms.

Contents

5 How to Use this Book

6 Introduction

9 Step By Step
By Renée Goularte
Introducing multi-age classes into a traditional school environment can be a risky undertaking. This teacher describes her mistakes and successes on the road to multi-age teaching. Learn how she successfully created a collaborative curriculum for first and third graders.

21 Classroom Buddies
By Patty LaRosa and Mary-Ellen Moon
Worried that older kids will be left behind in a multi-age environment? These teachers used a buddy system to ease first graders into their multi-age classes, and turn third graders into leaders and mentors.

33 When Students Resist
By Kristie Colwell-Cornett, Monica R. Louderback-Gibson, and Chanda E. Napier
What happens when sixth graders balk at sharing a classroom with fourth graders? Multi-age classrooms pose unique challenges at the middle-school level. Here's how flexible student grouping and cooperative learning techniques helped these teachers meet that challenge.

43 Sailing the Sea As We Build the Boat
By Debra Hime and Carolyn Moore
When student retention rates soared at Travis Heights Elementary school, a multi-age program was put in place. Today, students learn and progress at their own developmental pace. The retention rate is now zero.

59 Teaming for Success
By Kris Clark
Students aren't the only ones who benefit from multi-age groupings. Teachers at two Virginia elementary schools found that team teaching in multi-age classes put an end to classroom isolation, and spurred teacher support networks.

71 Multi-Age From the Ground Up
By Bobbie Faulkner and Patricia Faiveley
Scottsdale, Arizona, built its newest elementary school around a multi-age program that thrives on integrated thematic teaching, and the latest research in cognitive learning and multiple intelligences.

89 Selected Resources

94 Glossary

How to Use this Book

Multi-Age Classrooms is no ordinary book. It is one of a series from NEA Teacher-to-Teacher Books in which classroom teachers speak directly to other teachers—like you—about their school restructuring efforts.

Printed in the upper right-hand corner of every book cover in the series, is a routing slip that encourages you to pass the book on to colleagues once you have read it—in other words, to spread the word about school change.

Book topics cover areas such as large-scale school change, student assessment, authentic learning, inclusion, and time strategies.

Read the Six Stories

Inside each book you will find stories from six or more teachers across the country who discuss, step by step, how they tackled a specific restructuring challenge. They describe what worked and didn't work, and provide you with diagrams, checklists, or tables they think other teachers would find useful.

Write Your Own Ideas In This Book

At the end of each story in this book is an area called Reader Reflections. This area is for you and any colleague who reads the story to write related insights and action points for your school or school district to consider.

You see, the purpose of NEA Teacher-to-Teacher Books is not only to spread the word about school change, but to encourage other teachers to participate in its exploration.

Discuss Your Thoughts With Others

Once you have routed a book through your school, you can meet with colleagues who contributed to the Reader Reflections sections and expand upon your thoughts.

Go Online

Believe it or not, the communication and sharing does not have to stop there. You can discuss a Teacher-to-Teacher book series topic with teachers across the country. Any NEA member who subscribes to the America Online electronic network can participate in an ongoing forum on these book topics.

The National Education Association's area on the network is called NEA Online. Once signed on to NEA Online, just keyword to: *NEA Prof Library*.

To subscribe to NEA Online, call 1-800-827-6364 (NEA members should give preferred customer # 0437).

Introduction

"We have never worked harder, but we have never enjoyed our classes more."

This quote from elementary school teacher Bobbie Faulkner says it all. Teaching students of different ages together in the same classroom is hard work—-but oh so rewarding. Multi-age classrooms require tremendous planning. Teachers have to develop innovative curricula to match the various learning levels in the classroom. Classrooms must be organized and set up to encourage cooperative learning groups. And, there are always skeptical parents to appease.

But the rewards are immense. There's no greater feeling than watching a shy third grader emerge from her cocoon to help a first grader read. Or what about that five-year-old boy who, when asked what he's learning in kindergarten, responds, "I'm not in kindergarten, I'm in multi-age and I'm learning about books and oceans and how to get along with my friends!"

As you read the stories in this book, you'll find that multi-age classes and mixed-age groupings take many forms. Your multi-age program will differ depending on the circumstances and resources present in your school. And it really is an ever-evolving process.

The six stories in this book describe the many challenges and joys of multi-age teaching, from parent backlash to school district support and praise.

Parent Misunderstanding

Teachers Bobbie Faulkner and Patricia Faiveley tell how Scottsdale, Arizona, built its newest school—Aztec Elementary—on a foundation of multi-age teaching and integrated thematic instruction. When Aztec announced its multi-age grouping structure, some parents of older kids worried curriculum would be "watered" down to meet the needs of younger students. This story illustrates the importance of a strong parental education program in a multi-age environment. Faulkner and Faiveley also list and describe the many learning theories used to build their multi-age program, from Howard Gardner's theory of Multiple Intelligences to Bloom's Taxonomy.

Separate and Unequal

What happens when only part of a school goes multi-age? At Travis Heights Elementary School conflict arose between multi-age teachers and single-grade teachers. Single grade teachers expressed resentment when multi-age teachers received additional money for materials and release time for planning. Students and parents complained of unequal treatment when multi-age classes began using alternative assessments. Eventually, the entire school went multi-age. Teachers Debra Hime and Carolyn Moore call their journey into multi-age teaching, "sailing the sea as we build the boat." Rough waters aside, these teachers have developed a multi-age program that cut student retention rates and spurred innovative assessment practices.

Middle Grade Challenges

Multi-age groupings pose special challenges in the middle-grade levels. When sixth graders at Willard School in Kentucky balked at sharing a classroom with fourth and fifth graders, teachers knew they had to do something. Three middle grade teachers at Willard describe how they set up a flexible, cooperative learning program that encouraged students to appreciate and depend on each other. They also detail how curriculum is designed to meet the needs of each grade level.

Learning From Our Mistakes

Renée Goularte, a third grade teacher in San Jose, California, set up the perfect structure to get her multi-age classroom off the ground—or so she thought. Goularte describes how an elaborate setup of learning centers initially failed to get first, second, and third graders working together. There are great lessons to be learned in her step-by-step process.

When Teachers Team

There's no lack of research extolling the benefits of multi-age teaching on student performance. But students are not the only ones who benefit. Kris Clark describes how multi-age classes at two elementary schools in Alexandria, Virginia, led to the development of teaching teams. Those teaching teams brought about a spirit of collegiality and professional support among school instructors.

Building a Buddy System

Something wonderful is happening at White Rock School in Gorham, Maine. Nine-year-olds organize and run reading groups for seven- and eight-year-olds. Third graders help first graders with their spelling skills. Teachers Patty LaRosa and Mary-Ellen Moon detail how creative scheduling and learning workshops turned groups of first, second, and third graders into classroom learning buddies.

Concluding Thoughts

Multi-age classrooms are mushrooming in schools around the country. The six stories in this book just scratch the surface of what is occurring in this area of increasing popularity. But, if you're a teacher about to embark on the multi-age journey, you'll learn from the mistakes these teachers candidly admit they made. And, if you're already teaching in a multi-age environment, I hope you will come away with new strategies and tips to increase the success of your multi-age program. Finally, we end this book with an extensive list of resources to guide you to other activities and research in the area of multi-age teaching.

—Karen Gutloff
Series Editor

Notes:

_____

_____

_____

_____

_____

STEP BY STEP

Introducing multi-age into a traditional school environment is a challenging experience filled with highs and lows.

1 One thing my partner and I often do in our classroom is stand off to the side and observe. We stand close enough to the children to hear their conversations, but far enough away to be out of their learning space. Watching pairs of first and third graders read to each other, talk about the stories they've read, then work individually on written literature responses, continually assures me my most important job as teacher is to set up an environment for "real" learning—a place where students discover their own autonomy and learn how to help each other. Just like real life. Every day in our classroom, students of different ages interact naturally. But it wasn't always this way. It has taken us a year and a half of trial and error to get to this point.

I am a third grade teacher. I began my work in education many years ago at the junior high and high school level. I be-

RENÉE GOULARTE
Third Grade Teacher
Blossom Valley School
San Jose, California

came interested in teaching in a multi-age classroom ever since my own children—now teenagers—attended a Montessori school as young children. In that school children between ages 6 and 12 learned in the same classroom. I obtained a second credential and began teaching third grade in public school six years ago. I brought with me the desire to create an environment similar to the multi-age classrooms taught in the Montessori school. I quickly discovered my ideas were very different from most of the other teachers in my school, which had a strong traditional atmosphere. Even though I worked mostly alone, I began to pair up with a kindergarten teacher for weekly cross-grade math activities. I wanted more cross-grade activities, but wasn't sure how much I could do on my own.

Oak Grove School District, where I now teach, is in the southern area of

San José, California. It is a suburban district with a diverse student population from a wide range of socioeconomic levels. In my classes, I have had students whose parents' education levels range from high school dropouts to Ph.D. recipients. Oak Grove School District, like many others, has made deep financial cutbacks in the last few years. One of the results in the classroom has been the creation of more combination classes, partly as a way to hire fewer teachers. Many teachers at my school have viewed these combination classes in a negative light. I have welcomed and enjoyed working with these mixed grades, and have tried different strategies for teaching two grades as one.

When I met Ziem Nguyen, a bilingual first grade teacher who moved into the classroom next to mine, I began to discuss with Ziem my ideas about multi-age classes. Ziem and I traded ideas and discovered we shared mutual goals. By spring, we were talking informally about starting a multi-age classroom.

Research on Multi-Age Classes

As part of my masters' degree program, I began doing research. In study after study, I read about many academic and social benefits of mixed-age groupings. Many researchers had found that students in mixed-age groups performed as well or better than students in traditional, single-grade classrooms. The research showed students in mixed-age classrooms developed positive attitudes about school and improved social skills. I compared these readings with my own students' experiences in the combination classes I had taught, where students had learned to work together regardless of age or grade. Ziem and I felt confident that by starting a multi-age classroom, we would be creating a valuable program that could meet the varied developmental and academic needs of our first and third grade students. The only thing to do was figure out how to begin.

Combining Three Into One

In fall of 1993, I was teaching a second/third grade combination class. Ziem and I explained to the principal that we wanted to combine Ziem's first grade class with my 2/3 class. With the principal's support, we enthusiastically began moving forward. First, we decided to mix our students while still maintaining two separate classrooms. We began with something we called "flow time," when students could choose activities and work freely in either classroom. We were sure our students would naturally flow—

I watched one of my students, a child who is generally angry and sullen with his peers, teach his buddy place value concepts using a gentle manner that caught me by surprise.

hence the name—from one room to another and back again. But the students did not flow back and forth. The environment we created was artificial and just did not work. Most of my students stayed in "our" room and most of Ziem's students stayed in "their" room.

Next, we tried learning centers. These centers quickly became complicated and time-consuming to plan, because we wanted the students to be heterogeneously grouped, with a balance of ages, grades, gender, and academic levels. Plus, the centers needed to meet the needs of a wide range of learning styles and academic levels, in addition to covering all curricular areas. The students worked successfully together, but it was still an artificial system, more teacher-driven and contrived than we wanted. As much as the students enjoyed working together, we still did not see much natural movement. Some kind of inertia seemed to keep the students in their "own places."

When Students Stick to Their Turf

To stimulate student interaction, we developed a weekly "catch-up time," when students were to complete any unfinished work and check it with other students. But somehow the first graders, found it hard to use each other for resources. Ziem and I even tried declaring ourselves off limits during this time, telling the children to "go ask another student" to answer some of their questions. We wanted to use some of this time to discuss student progress and plan future activities. But the students came to us for help anyway. It wasn't working.

We continually reminded students they could take their work anywhere in either room. We told first graders to have second or third graders check their work before bringing

What Research Says About Multi-Age Groupings

In 1993 Robert Anderson, an elder statesman in school restructuring, and Barbara Nelson Pavan, a Temple University professor of educational administration, published *Nongradedness: Helping It To Happen*. In their book, Anderson and Pavan summarize 25 years of research, pointing to the effectiveness of multi-age classrooms:

There is now definite research evidence to confirm the theories underlying nongradedness. We are able to bring together for analysis the substantial and generally favorable body of research on nongradedness. Research studies published between 1968 and 1990 most frequently favored nongradedness on standardized measures of academic achievement and mental health. The results on academic achievement demonstrate that 58 percent of the studies have nongraded students performing better; 33 percent, the same; and only 9 percent worse than graded students. As to the mental health and school attitudes, 52 percent of the studies indicate nongraded schools as better, 43 percent similar, and only 5 percent worse than graded schools....

Boys, blacks, underachievers, and students of lower socioeconomic status were more likely to perform better and to feel more positive toward themselves and their schools in a nongraded environment. The longer pupils were in nongraded programs, the greater the improvement in their achievement scores in relation to ability....Thus research findings on nongraded, multigraded, and ungraded groupings of pupils generally support the use of these organizational arrangements in schools.

Excerpted from the book Nongradedness: Helping It To Happen, *Robert Anderson and Barbara Nelson Pavan, Technomic Publishing, 1993.*

it to the teacher. Ziem and I worked to convince all the students they now had two teachers and one classroom. In spite of what we said or did to reinforce this, all the students stuck to what they apparently understood was their own turf.

Assessing What Went Wrong

Before the end of the year, Ziem and I were frustrated, so we began analyzing what had not worked. This analysis would help us decide how to start over the next year. We spent a lot of time making lists of things that had worked and those that had not. We wrote down our goals, prioritized them, then made some decisions according to these priorities. We agreed one of the main problems the previous year was our inability to get students to interact without our direction. We needed to find ways to make the students comfortable with each other right away. This became our first priority. One thing we knew for sure was having two separate classrooms was a definite obstacle.

Back on Course

In June we submitted a request to have the walls separating our classrooms removed. Our principal, still supportive of our efforts, approved the request. By July, the walls were gone. The first time I saw that gaping hole, I thought, "Well, this is a little scary."

In the fall of 1994, Ziem and I began a fresh start. By then, however, we did not have enough second graders to move into the combination class. Ziem and I decided to proceed with a first-third grade combination.

In our workdays before the new school year began, Ziem and I consolidated our teaching materials and set up one large, common classroom. All of our language materials were put in one area. We set up our mathematics materials in another area. Social studies books for both grades were arranged on the same bookshelf. Art materials were stored together in open shelves for anyone to use. We set up only one calendar area, and created three clear, separate spaces for whole-group lessons and read-aloud story time. That setup would allow Ziem and me to have simultaneous grade-level class discussions that would not be disruptive to the other group.

Classroom Management

After creating the physical arrangement of the classroom, we discussed classroom management. There were many things we needed to make decisions about including clean-up, storage, distribution of playground equipment, discipline, seating arrangements, and general classroom procedures.

To encourage natural movement of students within the classroom, we decided they would not have assigned seats. Third graders would store their materials and work in crates, using hanging files for paperwork, while first graders would store theirs in cubbies.

> *Ziem and I have been open and flexible enough to stop and change direction when needed.*

We looked at curriculum and planned common themes for the entire year, based on the units in the first and third grade social studies texts. For the first two weeks of school, we combined all the students in one team-building collaborative activity each day, usually first thing in the morning. These were mainly physical education or other movement activities that immediately engaged the interest of all the students and totally avoided any need for grade-level separation. Students began to get to know one another. Once we got through those first two weeks, we began more sophisticated curriculum planning.

Collaborative vs. Single-Grade Curriculum

Neither Ziem nor I felt the need to overhaul everything all at once. We felt that doing one thing at a time would be easier for us, more beneficial for the students, and less confusing to parents who were used to a more traditional arrangement. We agreed we would each be responsible for our own grade-level curriculum, and we would collaborate on activities whenever possible. Essentially, what we were setting up was two separate grades within one classroom, with a crossover collaborative strand.

We devised a general curriculum for the year that covered language arts, mathematics, science, and social studies. We set up a sequential, September-June plan for first and third grade skills and units. Then we designed collaborative activities for each month that cut across all four curricular areas and addressed these skills. As complicated as this might sound, it actually took us only two hours. We use this matrix as our guideline for lesson and activity planning.

During the first months of our new program, Ziem and I spent many hours talking about what was working and what was not, and making decisions

Ten Tips for Starting A Multi-Age Classroom

1. Choose a partner you trust both personally and professionally.
2. Be willing and ready to compromise.
3. Make yourself knowledgeable about research on multi-age classrooms, and build a network of other teachers from whom you can get ideas.
4. Set clear, long-range goals, and realistic short-term goals.
5. Make sure your classroom environment matches your goals.
6. Build planning time into your schedule. Sacrifice something else, if you need to.
7. Constantly assess where you are in relationship to your short-term goals.
8. Be sure to assess failures and successes honestly. When something doesn't work, figure out why and try something different.
9. Ask the students, over and over again, what works for them.
10. Communicate with parents often about classroom activities. Invite them to observe or help in the classroom.

about what to do next. We thought carefully about curriculum that might lend itself to cross-grade collaboration, and that would be better suited to single-grade lessons. We slowly implemented many collaborative, cross-grade activities. We planned at least one regularly-scheduled cross-grade activity in each of the four main curricular areas. Most of these activities were scheduled once a week.

We grouped students

Other teachers have expressed fears that our multi-age class will "get all the good kids."

a variety of ways for different activities. For example, half of my students switched with half of Ziem's students once a week. Ziem took one mixed-age group to the library while I worked on music and movement activities with the other half of the students. One of the first weekly activities we introduced was collaborative reading. Pairs of first- and third-grade buddies read to each other, talked about the stories they read, then worked individually on written literature responses. Also once a week, third graders introduced their first grade partners to math concepts such as place value, trading, or number relationships, using manipulatives. These activities gave the third graders the opportunity to reinforce and practice concepts and skills, and helped them develop nurturing behaviors.

The Payoff: First- and Third-Grade Buddies

As we observed our students working together in pairs and small groups, we saw some interesting dynamics take place. One day I listened to a third grader's frustration when his buddy was not paying attention to a story. Another day, I watched one of my students, a child who is generally angry and sullen with his peers, teach his buddy place value concepts using a gentle manner that caught me by surprise. It is one thing to read about the development of social skills in multi-age groupings, but it is quite another thing to watch it happen right in your own classroom.

One of the most difficult obstacles Ziem and I faced was finding enough time for planning, which was and continues to be one of the most important elements of our program. When we had time to plan, everything seemed to run pretty smoothly. When we did not have time, we sometimes had a tendency to start drifting back into a "single-grade" mode.

Because we implemented several regular, weekly cross-grade activities, there is now a pleasant balance of single-grade and cross-grade groupings. It seems that we are finally beginning to observe a natural flow among students.

Benefits for Students/Teachers

Although our program might not work for every child, every parent, or every teacher, we are pleased with the general feedback to what we have done so far. Our students enjoy working in fluid groups, and have learned collaborative problem-solving strategies that meet the needs of their different ages and developmental levels. Third graders are developing leadership qualities while first graders are getting more challenges than they would in a single-age environment.

Ziem and I have learned how to compromise and help each other with personal as well as teaching goals. Parents have been very supportive for the most part; we receive many positive comments about the environment we have created.

Getting School Staff On Board

Multi-age classrooms are not a new idea, but they are unfamiliar to many parents and teachers, even though more are starting them. Since Ziem and I were working alone, without the active support of an entire school, our step-by-step implementation worked very well for us. It has given us the benefit of educating ourselves, parents, and colleagues a little at a time. Our principal, Risa Quon, has been very supportive of our efforts. She has encouraged other staff members to attend conferences about multi-age classrooms. She encouraged Ziem and me to formally present information about our plans to the school staff.

Although we enjoy great support from our principal, a number of our teaching colleagues have questioned the merits of our combination class. As I mentioned earlier, Blossom Valley is an extremely traditional school. Some teachers are just not convinced about the value of multi-age classrooms. Many express worry that our success with combination classes will force them into something they're not ready for. Other teachers have expressed fears that our multi-age class will "get all the good kids." And some teachers simply don't believe the research extolling the academic benefits of multi-age groupings.

Not all of our colleagues are skeptical though. A few of our fellow teachers occasionally ask questions about our progress. These colleagues have been very supportive. One teacher has asked to join us when we are ready to expand, and she has done some planning with us.

Ziem and I have made many mistakes along the way, but we have both

> *We agreed that one of the problems the previous year was our inability to get students to interact without our direction.*

been open and flexible enough to stop and change direction when needed. By taking the time to periodically assess what is working and what isn't, we are able to move steadily forward without becoming overwhelmed.

Toward Full Multi-Age

Now that we have reached the point where we are all starting to feel like one big class of sixty students with two teachers, Ziem and I are moving into a new phase. We are finding ways to ensure that we are viewed by the rest of the school as one classroom. We are working on changing lunch and recess schedules, which do not always match for us. We'd also like such things as school pictures and other activities to reflect our status as one class, not two.

Ziem and I are still in the process of finding new ways to combine all the students in collaborative activities designed to meet the needs of both grade levels. And we have begun to plan more total-group lessons.

> *Essentially, what we were setting up was two separate grades within one classroom, with a crossover collaborative strand.*

We plan to form cross-grade groups for reading and writing, and do more thematic lessons. We are also beginning to work with each others' students, which is helping us, as well as the students, solidify that sense of being one class.

Ziem and I have started making plans for next year. We are interested in eventually establishing a nongraded primary classroom where students would stay with us for three years. That should result in less transition time at the beginning of each school year. We are focusing on the steps we need to go through to achieve this long-range goal. We are meeting with our principal and district administrators about the possibilities.

District administrators have visited our program and expressed a great deal of support and enthusiasm about what we are doing.

We are talking about keeping most of Ziem's first graders next year, but also bringing in new first and third graders. We hope to have the class divided equally among first, second, and third graders. If we can do this, we can develop a second grade strand for our curriculum and skills matrix, and keep the first and second graders for a third year. Looking beyond to the third year, we envision a three-year primary program made up of students who enter at first grade and exit ready for fourth grade.

Now that our long-term goal seems closer to reality, we are planning our next steps with optimism and confidence. ◆

Single Grade vs. Collaborative Language Arts

	SEPT.	OCT.	NOV.	DEC.	JAN.	FEB.	MAR.	APR.	MAY
1st Grade	Word sounds	Differences between fiction and nonfiction	Sentence structure	Finding beginning, middle, and end of story	Capitalization, proper nouns, nouns vs. verbs	Adjectives	Writing, revising, editing stories	Writing, revising, editing stories	Writing, revising, editing stories
3rd Grade	Writing complete sentences	Writing story synopsis	Proofreading story	Study story characters	Writing dialogue	Basic story elements; write stories	Analyze and revise stories	Bookmaking	Bookmaking
Collaboration	Read aloud stories together	3rd graders read to 1st graders	1st graders ask 3rd graders questions about stories	3rd graders check 1st graders' work	3rd graders check 1st graders' work	3rd graders ask 1st graders questions about stories	Collaborative writing	Collaborative writing	Collaborative writing

Multi-Age Reproducible 1.2

Collaborative Reading for First and Third Graders

1. Choose an appropriate book.
2. Sit together.
3. Read the book.
4. Discuss the book.
5. Fill out top of reading form.
6. Illustrate or write about the story.
7. Check work with buddy.
8. Thank your buddy.
9. Share your work with a teacher.

Reader Reflections

Insights: _____

_____

_____

_____

_____

_____

Actions for Our School (District) to Consider: _____

_____

_____

_____

_____

_____

_____

_____

_____

CLASSROOM BUDDIES

A classroom buddy system can gently ease younger students into a multi-age environment, while turning older students into leaders and mentors.

Mandy, Beth, and Amy, all nine-years-old, are three very competent readers. They frequently read the same book—usually a very challenging one. They each keep a journal and design a book response project when they are finished. At the same time, Mandy, Beth, and Amy also like to organize and run "reading groups" for seven- and eight-year-olds in their classroom. One of them will hold up a set of multiple copies of a book and ask, "Who wants to be in the *Frog and Toad Are Friends* group?" There are always plenty of eager participants at a variety of reading levels. The girls help the younger students with decoding, talk about the meaning of new words, and teach the strategies they use as readers. They also ask comprehension questions, create packets to go with the books, and have "their" students respond in writing and drawing to what they've read.

This cooperative learning is one of the biggest joys of multi-age teaching at White Rock School in Gorham, Maine.

Gorham is a mixed-bag community. It's longtime agricultural identity is increasingly offset by its growth as a suburb of Portland, Maine. With this growth has come an influx of young families

PATTY LAROSA
Elementary teacher, grades 1-3
MARY-ELLEN MOON
Elementary teacher, grades 1-3
White Rock School
Gorham, Maine

seeking a pleasant town to live in, and good schools for their children. The Gorham School Department currently serves 2,200 students, representing a wide range of socio-economic backgrounds in kindergarten through grade 12.

White Rock is the smallest school in the system with 165 first, second, and third grade students in multi-age classrooms. It is located ten miles from the center of town in a still predominantly rural area. White Rock shares a principal with the districtwide

Kindergarten Center. Teachers here have—by design and necessity—relied on their own resources to solve problems and create change. We have worked hard to develop a professional culture that supports risk taking, mutual respect, and an open exchange of ideas. We also like to keep a sense of humor about us and maintain the joy of teaching and learning with young children.

Change has not always come easy. But we are fortunate to have a principal with high expectations, courage, and a great deal of faith in the expertise of classroom teachers. Our principal Sandy Price has guided our transition to a multi-age school. She has removed obstacles in our path, found scarce money, and fostered parent communication.

Long before we developed the first multi-age program at White Rock, classroom practices were changing. Whole language and literature-based reading were replacing basals and ability-based reading groups throughout the building. Children were using the writing process to keep journals and publish books. Pattern blocks, unifix cubes, microscopes, and magnifying glasses replaced textbooks on the shelves. At one time or another, monarch caterpillars, tadpoles, or chicken eggs were metamorphasizing, growing feet, or hatching in incubators. Throughout, we engaged in conversation with many teachers both within and outside our school about developmentally appropriate teaching and what it really looked like in the classroom.

We began to suspect that our classroom structures did not accommodate changes in our thinking about teaching and learning. We wondered how we could create more child-centered classrooms in which a wider range of talents and abilities would be at home. We questioned whether the yearly trade-off of students was serving the best interests of students, parents, or teachers.

In Search of Multi-Age Models

The notion of starting a multi-age program began to take shape through our ongoing dialogue with other teachers; extensive reading on early childhood education; and participation in many conferences, workshops, and classes. We also visited other schools, particularly the few multi-age programs that were in our area at the time. We liked what we saw in those programs. We especially liked the interactions among students, the diversity of learners, the students' self-direction and decision making, and the idea of students remaining with their teacher for two or three years. While we did not deny that those qualities

Children did not think multi-age grouping was all that unusual. Their classroom had just caught up with the rest of their lives.

could be built into traditionally grouped classrooms, we felt multi-age grouping enhanced them. Multi-age grouping also pushed teachers to develop instructional strategies and provide learning experiences for a wide range of interests and abilities.

Developing an Action Plan

The design for our program evolved over an eight-month period. Early in the planning process we applied for a state grant. The grant application called for us to describe our program and the rationale behind it. Despite our failure to win any grant money that year, the application process was invaluable in forcing us to bring our scattered ideas into focus and develop a plan of action.

Our initial plan called for the creation of a team-taught, multi-age second and third grade program. In this program, we would act as two teachers of approximately 40 students who would stay with us for two years. We saw great potential for getting to know our students better, developing stronger relationships with families, and becoming more effective collaborators.

Our major goal was to better meet the needs of all students and build classroom environments that supported many different types of learners and their talents. We were, and still are, particularly influenced by Howard Gardner's theory of multiple intelligences and the thinking that people can be smart in many ways. Gardner suggests that early elementary education should emphasize opportunity because intelligences are manifested in different ways at different developmental levels. Similarly, we wanted a program designed for differences in ability and maturity and less bound to grade level and chronological age. Other goals we identified revolved around relationships among children, and between children and adults. We wanted to en-

Before You Start

- **Research** the wide range of material available on multi-age grouping. It will help you develop your knowledge base and support your position.

- **Visit** multi-age programs in your area and talk to teachers about the philosophy behind multi-age grouping, as well as the nuts and bolts of the operation.

- **Look** closely at your curriculum and classroom practices. Decide if they are open ended enough to accommodate a wider span of abilities. Although different children may be involved with different tasks, you will not want to implement two parallel programs.

- **Involve** parents in the planning process early on. They will offer great insight and will be instrumental in garnering the support of other parents.

- **Develop** a clear vision of what you want your program to look like and articulate a plan of action for getting there. While this need not be cast in stone, it will give you confidence in starting out.

- **Offer** parent information nights. You will very likely have people who are resistant to changing how children are grouped. It is your responsibility to share your knowledge.

- **Invite** parents into the classroom as volunteers or just to see how the program works.

- **Ask** parents for feedback and their impression of the program.

- **Observe** your students carefully. Take notes and keep anecdotal records.

hance the qualities of cooperation, leadership, and decision making in the classroom. Developmental theorist, David Elkind, and education reformers, John Goodlad and Roland Barth, among others, contributed to our thinking.

Parent Enthusiasm, Skepticism

Implementation of our program began with parent information nights in, early Spring, before beginning the placement process the following school year. There was a great deal of interest, many questions, and some misconceptions. The most common misconception confused multi-age grouping with lack of classroom structure. Although we tried to relieve this with as much concrete information as possible, some skepticism remained. We had decided not to place children in the program against their parents' wishes during the pilot year, if possible. As it turned out, we had more than enough volunteers. Parents chose the program for a variety of reasons.

Some parents liked the idea of their children staying with the same teacher for a second year. Others saw the potential in mixing the ages of children in the classroom. A few had fond memories of attending school in one-room schoolhouses in rural Maine where multi-age grouping had been the norm. Several parents were interested in the option of a "nontraditional" classroom environment. Conversely, some parents were simply not interested in their children being the "guinea pigs" in a pilot program. By offering parents an option in the first few years of the program, we were able to build considerable support for the practice of multi-age grouping.

We dedicated that summer to designing curriculum and learning environments in our two adjoining classrooms. Although we tried to anticipate the potential problems, we had no idea what the first day of school would bring. What we worried about the most, came to pass the least.

Creating a Community of Learners

Today, the children in our multi-age class meld very naturally. The scene described earlier with Mandy, Beth, and Amy is typical of the kind of cooperative learning we see each day. The younger children are not intimidated by the older children. The older children do not act bossy or mean. They simply do not think being in a class with kids of different ages is all that unusual. In fact, their classroom has just caught up with the rest of their lives. In their families,

We wanted a program designed for differences in ability and maturity and less bound to grade level and chronological age.

their neighborhoods, churches, ball teams, and scout groups they are always involved with kids of other ages.

We continually stress the development of our classroom as a community of learners. We focus on the rights of individuals, as well as responsibility to the group. We impress upon students the need to use each other as resources. Each day begins with a whole-group meeting, which we use to share news, discuss the day ahead of us, and take care of business.

Our daily schedule is broken into extended time blocks or workshops on math, reading, and writing. Other workshops are devoted to our current theme of study or special projects. During projects, the children choose activities they want to engage in and decide who they want to work with. Since they have weekly obligations, they also choose how to budget their time and fulfill their responsibilities.

The choice of activities is as diverse as the members of the group: art projects, writing, computer work, research, reports, skills practice, and so on. We see many of the qualities we want to cultivate emerge strongly during projects. Our students exhibit problem solving and creative thinking as they decide what to do and how to do it. We see leadership and cooperation emerge as children work together on projects and negotiate rules and share materials. When given the opportunity to pursue their interests, the children are curious, creative, and express a willingness to learn. Their work easily crosses ages and grade levels. Children come to school with more interests than we can ever "teach" in a year. We have seven-year-old dinosaur experts, eight-year-old poets, and nine-year-old math fanatics. Our projects allow each child an opportunity to explore his or her interests more fully and share that expertise with others.

The Classroom Buddy System

We use formal cross-age partnerships to bring second and third graders together in working relationships. Over the years we have used classroom buddies, reading partners, writing partners, observation walk partners, and cooperative problem-solving groups. Some of these have stood the test of time and others have faded into oblivion as we have experienced how children naturally interact in the multi-age setting.

Our classroom buddy system, however, has become a fixture over the years. At the beginning of each year, the incoming students choose, or are matched up with, students that have been in the program for a year. The older buddies take the new kids under their wing and help them become acclimated to the program. Older buddies show their younger peers where materials are kept and how our classroom operates. The older chil-

It has not been our experience that the older students are "held back" in any way.

dren consider this an important job—a job they greatly anticipate in their second year.

MULTI-AGE CLASSROOMS ◂ **25**

Each morning, the buddies check in with one another to be sure that each has taken care of his or her morning responsibilities. Those responsibilities include buying lunch tickets or passing in notices. We do a "buddy check" at morning meeting when we take attendance. Some younger students tend to stick close to their older buddies through the first few weeks of school. They work side by side, read together, share snacks, and

Eight-year-old Stephanie is helping six-year-old Abbie develop a sight vocabulary.

play at recess. Soon, the younger students are comfortable in their new environment. They then work and play with the rest of the group.

Since we've expanded our second and third grade multi-age classrooms to include first grade, the buddy system has gained added significance. First graders are getting used to a whole new school, as well as a new teacher, classroom, and full-day program. Their older buddies contribute to a gentle transition. Our former students invariably mention their buddies as an important part of their years in the program.

Reading Buddies
It is important that cross-age partnerships are student-driven. For example, our partner reading project was initially structured as a reading workshop with us deciding when it would happen, for how long, and what it would look like. Gradually, we realized that we were limiting, rather than enhancing, the working partnerships between the children. As we became more comfortable with letting go of the control of reading workshops we saw wonderful things happen. The nine-year-olds like Mandy, Beth, and Amy began to assume leadership roles, teaching their younger peers how to decipher words, read, and analyze stories.

The wide span of reading skills represented in the classroom created a positive situation for children who had a more difficult time becoming able readers. Stephanie, a struggling eight-year-old, was able to get much-needed reading practice — without stigma attached. She read easy, repetitive, or predictable books to six-year-old Abbie. Stephanie was helping Abbie develop a sight vocabulary. She even had Abbie building a word bank on index cards.

Six-year-old Ben could not sit still for a minute. He had little interest in books or learning to read. Even ten minutes of silent reading was a chore for Ben until he met up with Peter. Peter began the year before in much the same way. The two boys found they share a passion for nature magazines. Given the opportunity, the boys would pore over the magazines for the whole day. With Peter's more developed reading ability, the boys could do more than look at the pictures. They worked hard at figuring out captions and began to read accompanying texts. They used their reading work in other class projects, creating posters and reports on snakes and

Maine animals.

Certainly not every child is involved in such rich partnerships all of the time. Independent reading, book conferences with adults, and literature groups with the teacher are all parts of a student's reading program. However, the value of their partnering cannot be understated. We have learned to draw on the diversity of their approaches and make them available to other children.

Writing Buddies

Similarly, our approach to partnering in the writing workshop has evolved over time. Here, we have seen even less connection to age or grade level, and more reflection of student interests and talents. Six-year-old Charlie was never at a loss for a story idea. Seven-year-old Christie was a master at illustrating. And eight-year-old Bridget was adept at spelling and using the dictionary. The children drew upon one another as the need arose. They spent much less time waiting for an adult and more time engaged in writing.

Developing collaborative student relationships is more a function of the culture of the classroom—indeed the whole school—than the result of our interventions. The multi-age setting appears to contribute to the development of such a culture.

Older Students Not Left Out

We regularly assess our students' attitudes about being in multi-age classrooms. We find students have positive attitudes about being helped by, or helping, other children in the classroom. According to one survey, the children reported they often turned to their peers for help, before seeking out a teacher. Collaboration benefits both older and younger students socially and academically. This is particularly important to us. While few people argue the benefits of multi-age grouping for the younger students, they question the benefits for the older students. It has not been our experience that the older students are "held back" in any way. They view themselves as successful learners and feel they have something to offer others. The documentation of their work in portfolios reflects steady academic growth. Their scores on standardized tests are consistent with those of their counterparts in traditionally grouped classrooms in the system.

Over the years, multi-age grouping has spread throughout our school building and now White Rock is a completely multi-age school. We encountered a pocket of resistance when we eliminated

We are particularly influenced by Howard Gardner's theory of multiple intelligences and the thinking that people can be smart in many ways.

the remaining self-contained classrooms two years ago. It was difficult for us not to personalize

MULTI-AGE CLASSROOMS 27

the negative reaction of a very small number of parents. But we persevered. We regularly offer parents schoolwide and classroom forums on multi-age grouping. We also encourage parents to come to school so they can see firsthand how these programs work. Again, a collaborative staff and a supportive administration have been crucial. But our greatest advocates have been the parents of children that have gone through the program. They are often more successful in easing the doubts of skeptical parents than we can hope to be. They have been successful in advocating for multi-age programs at the next grade levels.

We do not see multi-age grouping as a panacea for all the problems we encounter in schools. Our daily life in the classroom remains as challenging as ever. We have been gratified, however, to see that many of the goals we envisioned—student leadership, self-direction, resourcefulness, cooperation, and appreciation for diversity—are well ensconsed in our classrooms. ◆

By offering parents an option, we were able to build considerable support for multi-age grouping.

Multi-Age Reproducible 2.1

The Buddy System

We use formal cross-age partnerships to bring first, second, and third graders together in working relationships. Over the years we have used classroom buddies, reading buddies and writing buddies.

Our Buddy System

Creates opportunities for peer mentoring.

Gives younger students an immediate friend or guide who will show them the ropes and ease their fears.

Provides older students with an important "job" they anticipate.

Allows students with weaknesses to practice skills by working with partners.

Gives first graders a gentle transition into a new environment.

Promotes leadership skills in second and third graders.

Develops social skills among students.

Multi-Age Reproducible 2.2

Student-Driven Learning

It is important that cross-age partnerships are student-driven. In our classroom, students are actively involved in, and responsible for much of the learning experience:

In a student-driven learning environment:

Students choose activities they want to work on and decide who they want to work with.

Students have weekly obligations or academic goals to meet.

Students choose how to budget their time and fulfill their responsibilities.

Students use each other as resources.

Outcomes include:

Students exhibit problem solving.

Students show creative thinking.

Students begin to assume leadership roles.

Students engage in cooperative behavior.

Students express a willingness to learn.

Reader Reflections

Insights: ───────────────

──────────────────────────────
──────────────────────────────
──────────────────────────────
──────────────────────────────
──────────────────────────────

Actions for Our School (District) to Consider: ─────

──────────────────────────────
──────────────────────────────
──────────────────────────────
──────────────────────────────
──────────────────────────────
──────────────────────────────
──────────────────────────────
──────────────────────────────

WHEN STUDENTS RESIST

Three teachers describe how they overcame student resistance to multi-age groupings in the middle grades.

3 Willard School is located in Busy, Kentucky, a small, rural area in Perry County. In 1992, Willard School was chosen as one of 15 schools in Kentucky to participate in the National Alliance for Restructuring Education (NARE). Willard received this honor as a result of a determined effort to make education reform an integral part of our vision for successful students.

Our school serves approximately 350 students in kindergarten through the 8th grades. We have an all-inclusive program. Instead of pull-out classes, the Chapter 1 teachers, special education teachers, parent volunteers, and peer tutors work alongside each classroom teacher to meet the needs of every child.

Our primary and middle school students are organized into four learning teams. The three of us make up a teaching team (Team 3). We each specialize in a particular area. One teacher focuses on language arts, another on math, and the third on science. We all teach social studies. The majority of our students come from a low socioeconomic background, which often puts them at a disadvantage. Nonetheless, Willard School functions as the heart of the community and strives to open the door to opportunities that would not have been there otherwise.

KRISTIE COLWELL-CORNETT
Science Teacher, grades 4-6
MONICA R. LOUDERBACK-GIBSON
Math Teacher, grades 4-6
CHANDA E. NAPIER
Language Arts Teacher, grades 4-6

Willard School
Busy, Kentucky

Why Mix Middle Graders

There is something unique about Willard School. We place our students in multi-age, multi-ability settings. The Kentucky Education Reform Act (KERA), which became effective in July 1990, mandates nongraded classes for all primary grades. Each of us came into teaching just as nongraded

MULTI-AGE CLASSROOMS 33

primary classes were being implemented under KERA. We thought multi-age classes worked so well in the primary grades that we should extend this type of grouping throughout the middle school level as well. Our rational for this was the motivation and excitement seen in the primary students. They seemed to grasp the concept of collaborating and realized the unique qualities that each class member had to offer. Also, the test scores from the primary nongraded classes showed more effective learning was taking place.

There are particular advantages to mixed-aged groupings at the middle school level. All the students are at different physical, social, emotional, and intellectual developmental stages. Children reap many benefits from this diverse environment. Students see and learn about their own developmental changes by observing others. The students also learn how to interact positively with peers at different age and ability levels. This understanding prepares students for real-life situations.

We thought multi-age classes worked so well in the primary grades that we should extend this type of grouping throughout the middle school level as well.

Initial Concerns

Though we saw potential advantages of grouping fourth, fifth, and sixth graders, we still had a number of questions as we set out on our project. Some of those questions were:

1. Would such a large range of ages be compatible?

2. How would we cover three sets of curricula?

3. Would multi-age grouping push the fourth graders too hard?

4. Would sixth graders get enough academic stimulation?

5. Would parents and community members accept mixed-age groupings?

Overall, these concerns turned out to be unfounded. Through careful planning we were able to design student teams that took into account the academic and social compatibility of each child. We developed a curriculum that all students could participate in, regardless of their skills level. And, we encouraged parents to visit the classroom and observe how well their children learned in the multi-age environment.

Building Student Learning Teams

We began planning our first year of multi-age classes by looking at student-grouping patterns. First, we decided which grades to place in each team. Team One consists of kindergarten through second grade; Team Two, grades two through four; Team Three, grades four through six; and Team Four, grades six through eight. We group students into each team. We constantly revise teams to ensure a balanced mix of gifted, average, and lower-level ability students. We also consider the physical and social maturity of the students. To ward off possible problems we also look at prior personal conflicts among students.

Within our team, students are arranged in flexible, cooperative learning groups. We make a conscious effort to include in each group, students who are low-, middle-, and high-achievers. Students engaged in cooperative learning, peer tutoring, and individual tasks. At any given time we changed the group for various reasons. Some of our groupings include problem-solving groups, needs-requirements groups, needs-reinforcement groups, interest groups, and learning-style groups.

This kind of flexible grouping allows us to fully meet the needs of each child.

Flexible Curriculum and Assessment

A typical day for our class begins in homeroom, where students perform daily housekeeping chores. Each student then attends classes in language arts, mathematics, science, music, art, and physical education. Students also visit the library or receive guidance counseling. In the afternoon, the students return to homeroom for social studies. The day ends with flexible time, which includes math and writing portfolio refinement, exploratory courses, and enrichment activities.

During the actual classroom instruction, we assign students work based on their individual grade level. At other times, the whole class is given the same high-level assignments. However the lessons are assigned, students work at their own pace for a continuum of learning. When fourth graders begin to increase their skills, they advance within the curriculum. We also make lessons more challenging for fifth or sixth graders who develop skills more quickly.

When students are asked to do the same work, we make adjustments during assessment. We assess student performance using anecdotal records, open-response exams, performance events, and portfolios. The rubrics set up for each task vary in expectations for each grade. Students in sixth grade are held to a higher standard of accountability than those in fifth and fourth. Likewise, we have higher expectations for fifth grade than for those students at the fourth grade level. Although

Kentucky's Nongraded Primary

The Kentucky Education Reform Act (KERA) of 1990 established that each elementary school in the state would begin to implement an ungraded primary program during or before the 1992-1993 school year.

fourth grade is the lowest level in our multi-age team, the students are still held responsible for meeting high standards. All students in our multi-age block are encouraged to use their ability to the fullest in order to attain the highest level of achievement possible.

Student Resistance To Multi-Age Grouping

When we created our multi-age classrooms we set high goals for ourselves and our students. The goals we set for ourselves were to remain flexible and continually change grouping patterns to prevent student boredom. We also decided to not give up, even when things looked bleak.

Our goals for students were to interact with others effectively, share their knowledge, learn the importance of cooperation, and raise their test scores.

We envisioned a classroom utopia of learning and motivation. This, however, was not exactly the case during the first phases of implementation. Initially there was some resentment among students. For example, the sixth grade students questioned why they were in a

Sixth grade students questioned why they were in a class with fourth and fifth graders.

classroom with fourth and fifth graders. The sixth graders felt they were being held back. They did not understand how they could possibly glean anything positive from younger students. The fifth grade students were caught in the middle. They were the most indifferent toward multi-age grouping. Fourth graders felt intimidated and worried their work would be too difficult.

Changing Students' Attitudes

We devised a program to get each student actively involved in and responsible for their group's work. After about the first month of school our efforts began to pay off. Things started to fall into place and we were able to change student attitudes toward one another. When students worked in groups, we made sure each person had a specific role to play. When assignments were completed, we pointed out how important each student's role was in completing the task. Students began to realize they could not accomplish their task or goal alone. Sixth graders needed to rely on their younger peers and vice versa.

We began to watch students work more cooperatively together. If one student could not grasp a task or concept, another would pick up the slack. Overall, the fourth, fifth, and sixth graders began to understand they were not the beginning or the end, but a member of the whole, with individual talents to contribute. As students began to see the value each age level brought to the classroom environment, their attitudes changed. The following are quotes from students about their experiences in multi-age classrooms:

"I really like multi-age grouping. I think it's great for kids of different ages to cooperate together. It gives kids more benefit from what they learn. The class I'm in does fourth, fifth, and sixth grade. It's a whole lot better than one grade. I like helping others with their work. It's good to know that you can help someone younger than you learn something. Before I was in multi-age groupings I didn't like class. It was boring. Everyone except the teacher was the same age. Now I'm in a class with kids who are younger than me, and kids who are older than me. I like it a lot."
Eddie Dean Stacy, grade 5

"I think that multi-age grouping is a good thing because it helps people learn better. If we do sixth

grade work, fourth and fifth graders can learn things a lot faster. Or, if we do fourth or fifth grade work it could help the sixth graders because maybe they did not learn about that in fourth or fifth grade. I think it is better to have us in a multi-age group because everyone can help each other. Even fourth and fifth graders can help the sixth graders sometimes."

*Sue Holland,
grade 6*

Parents, Principal On Board

In order to have a successful multi-age classroom, there must be strong support from the principal. Our principal, Ruby Napier, is convinced multi-age grouping in the classroom has proven to be an invaluable stepping stone on the road to student achievement.

Parental support and involvement is also essential to the success of any multi-age program. Our parent volunteer program allows parents to come into the classroom and see first hand what their child is learning. Parent familiarity with student classroom work reinforces learning at home. This also enables parents to become a vital part of not only their child's education, but the school community as a whole. Parents then become much more comfortable with other reforms taking place within the school.

The Big Obstacle: Planning Time

The biggest problem we encountered in our multi-age program was insufficient planning time. We overcame this dilemma by working with our principal and the entire faculty.

We worked out a schedule that allowed each team to have a 45-minute common planning period each day. We also lengthened the school day Tuesday through Friday to compensate for a shorter student day on Monday. On Mondays, the students go home at 12:15 p.m. The rest of the day is used for common planning time within teams, or involving the entire school.

Looking Forward

Overall, we found the advantages of multi-age grouping far outweigh any dilemmas we encountered. The sixth grade students learn to help their younger peers with work. The older students also become role models. All students learn to socialize with others—a great preparation for real life. And, each student develops independent work habits.

Multi-Age = Continuous Progress

"Multi-age grouping is excellent because it helps with continuous progress. Students can learn at their own speed and do not have to stop—which would cause their learning to be stifled—just because they have mastered a certain grade level. This type of grouping also allows for adaptability and review for those students who have fallen behind. In life, we as adults are not constricted to time or age constraints in our learning. Multi-age grouping allows students to not be held back by these constraints as well."

—Ruby Napier
Principal, Willard School

As for the future of our multi-age, multi-ability classrooms in the middle school, we plan to continue our efforts and seek new ideas to increase success. One future goal is to align the curriculum and set exit criteria for each team in the school. This would assure us that students coming into their new block will have the basic skills necessary for their continuous progress in that learning team. ◆

Multi-Age Reproducible 3.1

How You Can Create a Successful Multi-Age Classroom

1. Provide a wide variety of reading material in the classroom. Be sure to include varying levels and interests.
2. Structure the day to provide time for peer tutoring among students.
3. Involve students when you plan lessons, themes, types of assessments, etc.
4. Integrate the curriculum as much as possible.
5. Use your support staff to the fullest. This includes special education teachers, Chapter I teachers, art teachers, music teachers, physical education teachers, librarians, and guidance counselors.
6. Do not put students into categories or track them. Allow them to learn at their own pace.
7. Use manipulatives when possible so as to compensate for differing ability levels.
8. Use a variety of assessment strategies.
9. Use various types of grouping patterns within the classroom to meet special needs such as: problem solving, learning styles, interests, etc.
10. In the beginning stages of implementation, give it time. Everything will not fall into place overnight. And BE FLEXIBLE!!

Grade 4-6 Classroom Schedule

MONDAY SCHEDULE	
7:30–7:45	Homeroom
7:45–8:45	Language Arts
8:45–9:25	Music (Homeroom)
9:25–9:45	Math
9:45–10:30	Science
10:30–10:45	Recess
10:45–10:55	Science
10:55–11:25	Lunch (Homeroom)
11:25–12:00	Social Studies (Homeroom)
12:00-12:10	Dismissal

TUESDAY–FRIDAY SCHEDULE • ROOM 8	
7:30-7:45	Homeroom
7:45-8:55	Language Arts
8:55-9:30	Math
9:30-10:15	Special Classes
10:15-10:30	Recess
10:30-11:05	Math
11:05-11:20	Science
11:20-11:45	Lunch
11:45-12:40	Science
12:40-1:40	Social Studies (Homeroom)
1:40-1:50	Snack
1:50-2:45	Flex Time
2:45-2:50	Dismissal

Cooperative Groupings for Multi-Age Classrooms

Within our teams, students are arranged in flexible, cooperative learning groups. At any given time these groups can be changed for various reasons.

Problem-Solving Group:
Students are brought together to discuss a common dilemma.

Needs-Requirements Group:
Students are instructed in a particular skill or concept.

Needs-Reinforcement Group:
Students receive additional work with specific topics or tasks.

Interest Group:
Student explore the same interests.

Learning-Style Group:
Students with a common pattern of learning work together.

Reader Reflections

Insights: _____

_____

_____

_____

_____

_____

Actions for Our School (District) to Consider: _____

_____

_____

_____

_____

_____

_____

_____

_____

SAILING THE SEA AS WE BUILD THE BOAT

How a two-year multi-age classroom cycle helped cut student retention rates at Travis Heights Elementary School.

4

We teach at Travis Heights Elementary in Austin, Texas, less than two miles from the state capitol. Our school serves a diverse population of students from a wide ethnic and socioeconomic spectrum. Within the two-mile radius of the school's boundaries are exclusive homes with historical landmarks, as well as motels along South Congress Avenue, where many of our families live on a week-to-week basis. Four government-subsidized housing apartment buildings are also nearby. Many of our students are recent immigrants, and come from families with little or no formal schooling. A number of our children also come from families led by very young mothers who are high school drop-outs. We also have students from intact families of skilled and professional parents.

DEBRA HIME
CAROLYN MOORE

Grades, 1-2

Travis Heights Elementary School

Austin, Texas

Who Has Failed? The Child or The System?

There are more than 60,000 students in the Austin School District. A few years ago we came face to face with a major problem in our district. Records showed 600 first graders had been retained. This was not an unusual failure rate by Austin's standards. The State of Texas similarly retains more than 10 percent of first graders. That adds up to 27,000 children held back annually. When our principal, Marilyn Butcher, first read the district statistics, she was appalled. There had to be something wrong with a system that retained so many seven- and eight-year-olds. When Marilyn checked the numbers for our school, she was shocked to find that Travis Heights had done its share of retaining first graders. We

MULTI-AGE CLASSROOMS ◀ 43

knew the first grade curriculum was not meeting the needs of these students, but we were not sure what to do about it. We noticed many first graders simply were not ready for the structured program that was in place.

For one thing, there was such culture shock in the transition from kindergarten to first grade. Rows of individual desks replaced small group centers, while stacks of pre-

It quickly became apparent that standard assessment practices were not going to work in our multi-age classroom.

primers and primers replaced hands-on science explorations. Secondly, there was pressure on first graders to plow through six required books. If a child managed to get through book six by May, he or she would advance to second grade. If the student fell short in reaching that goal—by a month or a year—the child was destined to repeat all of first grade. At the same time we had students who were ready to progress at a faster pace. Our first grade curriculum seemed pulled in too many directions. We discovered other grades were also feeling this academic crunch.

We began to look at multi-age classrooms as a solution to this retention problem. We set out to solve the problem by creating a multi-age classroom that would respect the diversity of student learning rates and styles. We hoped a multi-age program would ease the transition from kindergarten to first grade by allowing first graders to work at their own developmental pace. If a student didn't progress through the first grade curriculum by May, he or she could stay in the class until skills progressed. When a student became ready for more difficult work, he or she would receive higher-level work—within the same classroom. We would, in the process, eliminate the stigma and self-esteem problems that crop up when students are retained.

Year One—Diving In

We began our journey to multi-age by reading information on multi-age programs in the United States and Canada. We planned to study the concept for a year, and begin implementation in the fall of 1992. Our plans were pushed into fast forward, however, by circumstances that developed in our school in the fall of 1991.

We had too many students in grades one and two and needed to hire one more teacher. The problem: we had limited space for the new teacher and classroom. Our solution: three of us decided to combine our classes and become a team of multi-age 1-2 teachers. This was the beginning of an exciting journey. One parent accurately called it "sailing the sea as we built the boat."

Nonetheless we jumped in. We rearranged our classrooms, called parents, and wrote lesson plans—all over one weekend. Parents were apprehensive, but trusting and supportive. We set up several parent meetings and were very up front about what we saw as the benefits, the questions, and the "we don't knows."

We soon realized most of the parents' concerns stemmed from a lack of understanding about multi-age classrooms. Some were worried we would simply teach to the lowest common denominator. They thought all students would get the first grade curriculum. Other parents were afraid higher achieving students would go unrecognized and spend most of their time tutoring lower achieving students. A few parents even suggested that placement in the multi-age classroom was a kind of retention. Fortunately, these gross misunderstandings and negative feelings were limited to a very few. They surfaced early on among parents of the older students. Parent concerns quickly subsided as the effectiveness of our multi-age program began to show.

Creating An Environment Ripe for Learning

We learned many things in year one of our program. First, we reviewed the essential elements for first and second grade. There wasn't a tremendous amount of difference between the two, yet first grade seemed to progress at a breakneck pace, while second grade was more laid back. We decided our new multi-age 1-2 class would keep students with us for two years. We would not promote kids at the end of the first year. With a span of two years, kids who needed the extra time to become readers, would have it, with plenty of time to spare for the remainder of the curriculum.

Next, we borrowed some of that comfortable kindergarten culture for our class. We opened the accordion curtain separating the two classrooms, expanding our physical space. Rugs, blocks, rocking chairs, Legos, and centers replaced the old rows of desks. We brought a wide variety of "real books"—as many of the children refer to books outside the basal reader category—into the classroom.

Simply knowing we had two years instead of one with this new class, lifted that awful pressure from teachers and students alike. The two-year cycle allowed us to put our energies where they belonged—toward learning, at whatever pace.

We noticed immediately that while cooperative learning works nicely in the graded classroom, it is more fully realized in the multi-age classroom. Flexible grouping and re-grouping is easier with a wide range of ages and abilities. A true sense of community, and shared learning between teachers and students happens. The emphasis on collaboration and socialization that is central to cooperative learning is likewise a cornerstone in the multi-age classroom. Competition among students is replaced by a growing sense of community, with students and teachers sharing in each other's growth.

Parents Want Answers To These Questions:

- What should children know and be able to do within appropriate age levels?
- How is my child progressing toward the achievement of these goals?
- How is my child progressing toward mastering academic standards set by the state?
- How does my child's academic progress compare with his or her peers on a national scale?

Year Two—
The Payoff

Although we had learned a lot during our first year with a multi-age 1-2 class, the joy of the lessons learned during the second year lie at the heart of our multi-age program.

We had made many changes in our classroom that first year, yet at the end of May we still had students who were not reading, or were not where they were "supposed to be"—according to traditional standards. Our changes in classroom culture and teaching strategies had not in one year solved the retention problem. It wasn't until the first day of class the following year, that we began to harvest the fruits of our risk-taking adventure.

Returning parents confided in us that both they and their children had enjoyed the most relaxing summer ever, knowing they would be back with us in the fall. Returning second graders joined us in welcoming incoming first graders.

Within the first few weeks of the new year, we noticed breakthroughs with a number of students, which continued through the fall. For example, we had worked patiently with a student named Veronica during the first year on punctuation. We tried unsuccessfully to get her to put periods at the end of sentences. Her writing journal often looked like it had a bad rash. There were dots all over the place. In November of her second year, Veronica walked up to us, held out her journal entry, perfectly punctuated, with a capital letter at the beginning of each sentence, and said, "I got it!"

Rosemary, a second-year student with a similar problem in math, "got" place value under much the same circumstances in December. Many of our children who had not begun reading by May of their first year, picked up books sometime during the fall of the next year and read with skill, confidence, and—best of all—a great deal of joy. That joy was shared by teachers and fellow students. As teachers, it was incredibly gratifying to be able to witness these moments, to be there for each breakthrough. And, the sense of community that was evident when a child sincerely congratulated another child on becoming a reader, is something every teaching team and every student should get to experience.

Expanding
The Experience

In the Fall of 1992 we went along with a group of other teachers to Victoria, Canada, to visit multi-age classes. Canada had been using multi-age grouping for about twenty years. There, we saw evidence of kindergarten culture—including learning centers—at the middle school level! Our visit validated many of our philosophies and practices. Meanwhile, back home in Texas, nine more Travis Heights teachers joined their classes into a multi-age program. In ad-

Rugs, blocks, rocking chairs, Legos, and learning centers replaced the old rows of desks.

dition to our 1-2 class, there were now K-1, 2-3, 3-4, and 4-5 classes involving approximately one-third of the staff. The overlap in grades gave us flexibility when deciding where to group students.

A student could, for example, move from two years in a 1-2 class to a 2-3 (as opposed to a 3-4) if she or he needed more time with the second grade curriculum. The student would still be with chronological peers, but would have the extra time to master skills and concepts. This student would very likely spend only one year in this class, and then move on according to schedule. On the other hand, a very accelerated student could stay only one year in a 1-2 class, and finish elementary school a year early. In practice, most students go from a 1-2 to a 3-4, and so on. More than once, though, the arrangement has allowed a previously retained student to catch up with his or her peers. In at least four cases, parents of very bright students who could have moved after one year in a 1-2 to a 3-4 classroom, decided to have their child stay the two years with us, recognizing the needs of the whole child. While their academic skills were accelerated, their emotional maturity was right in line with what one would expect of seven-year-olds.

There were benefits for us teachers as well. With only three classes involved, it was easy for us to make adjustments as we went along. Teaming was something we became good at. We couldn't imagine ever teaching solo in an isolated classroom again.

Why Are We Making Changes In The Way We Assess Student Progress?

It has been said that if a time traveler from the turn of the century were to land in the 1990s, the only institution he would recognize would be the school. While tremendous changes have occurred in business, industry, etc., and we have moved from the industrial to the information age, schools have generally not kept up with the changing times.

At Travis Heights we are restructuring so that our school does indeed prepare students for the 21st century. The changes we are making in the assessment system are only one part of a larger change that involves teaching strategies (such as cooperative learning), school organization (multi-age groupings), and curriculum (thematic approach combining several disciplines). All of these are related and *support* one another.

Assessment is no longer "the test at the end of the chapter," but a *continuous* guide to instruction. Students assume more *responsibility* for their own achievement. Quality work becomes the standard and is celebrated for its *intrinsic* value. And parents become partners in increasing student achievement through increased understanding of the expectations.

Teacher Dissension

Though we realized many successes in the second year of the multi-age program, it was not all smooth sailing. By the time we started the second year of our program, a third of the school had followed our lead into multi-age classes. The term "slice academy" was used to refer to dedicating a cross-section of the school to multi-age classes. But soon "slice" became too accurate a description of what our expanded multi-age program was doing to the staff, students, and the community.

We had created two campuses. Teachers not

> **How and When Is Student Progress Reported To Parents?**
>
> **Period 1: Aug. 15 - Oct. 14**
> Parent Conference, Release Day—Oct. 19
>
> **Period 2: Oct. 17 - Dec. 16**
> Narrative reports—Dec. 16
>
> **Period 3: Jan. 3 - Mar. 3**
> Parent, Teacher, Child 3-Way Conferences—Mar. 8
>
> **Period 4: Mar. 6 - May 19**
> Narrative report, promotion information—May 19
>
> *Interim Reports are sent only to the parents of students experiencing major difficulties.*

taking part in the multi-age program were jealous when multi-age teachers received additional money for materials and release time for planning. Other teachers questioned our professional expertise, asking, "what do they know that we don't?" These professional misgivings could have been minimized if we had taken the time to communicate regularly with the rest of the staff. Students and parents also expressed strong feelings of unequal treatment when multi-age classes began using alternative assessments, including narrative reports and parent-student conferences.

For all of those reasons it was a relief to us when, in the Fall of 1993, the entire school went multi-age.

Adoption of a multi-age organization alone did not, of course, result in a true multi-age school in the short course of two years. Some teachers were reluctant. One even said to us, "You started this." (The sentiment was not one of deep gratitude.) As Madeline Hunter observed regarding multi-age, changing the organization only formalizes the expectation that teachers will recognize the many learning rates and skill levels within their classes. Our principal, Marilyn Butcher, created a game called "Find the Multi-Age Classes," based on reading comprehension test results during the second year of the project. It's obvious from this "game" that every class, whether a multi-age class or a traditional graded class, is in truth a multi-age class, when one considers the range of cognitive ages represented!

Assessment in A Multi-Age Environment

Changes in instructional strategies and assessment are as much a part of multi-age teaching as grouping children of various ages together in a classroom. It quickly became apparent to us that standard assessment practices were not going to work in our multi-age classroom. The whole philosophy was "everyone develops at different rates" and "we're here to work together, not compete." Some people became confused that the term nongraded—sometimes used synonymously with multi-age—meant no assessment. In fact, the opposite is true. In a multi-age classroom you are constantly assessing student progress, needs, and interests. To support this approach, we developed an alternative system of assessment. We report student progress every nine weeks using a combination of conferences and narrative reports. We don't give grades to students. This kind of change in our traditional grading system required dialogue with parents. We initiated parent meetings, called Open Forums, to allow informed discussion of the new system. With the help of involved and supportive parents, we put out booklets in English and Spanish, including

"Student Assessment at Travis Heights—A Parent's Guide," and "3-Way Conferences—A Child-Centered Approach to Sharing Student Progress with Parents." We learned that kids know what their best work is and they know what quality work is. Our expectation that they self-assess is the highest expectation we can have for them. Students are responsible for gathering and selecting work for their portfolios, which they share with their parents and teachers at the three-way conferences held in the spring. These student-led conferences are probably the most powerful element of the alternative assessment system. Students take them seriously, opening up their portfolios like an executive opening his or her briefcase for an important presentation. Parents—even those who showed initial resistance—are impressed with the content of the child's portfolio and the poise and confidence with which the child presents it. One child, whose parents were divorced, managed to talk his father into coming to school for the first time, to attend his three-way conference. The father, who showed little interest and signs of disapproval before the conference, came away from the event with a very positive attitude. He was really proud of his child's work. The student's behavior changed dramatically for the better after this experience. Once given to crying episodes, he became relaxed. School was okay. His dad approved.

Taking Stock

There are many indications that this journey, that began with certain elements of chance, is the right journey for us. Students have good attendance and exhibit positive social interaction. We have a zero retention rate. Cooperative learning has become a vital educational experience for students and teachers alike. Parents in general are pleased and supportive. Although a few have transferred out, there is a much longer list of families waiting to transfer in. The community seems to view us as an oddity that works. Our school has a solid reputation in our neighborhood as well as in our city.

There are still, however, some areas of concern. While most teachers understand and implement the multi-age philosophy, a few still teach from the textbook using grade-specific curriculum. Judicious use of teacher

The Three-Way Conference

The goals of the conference should be for *all those present:*

- to **learn** about the student's interests, habits and abilities
- to **reflect** on those interests, habits, and abilities
- to **set goals** to further develop those interests, habits, and abilities

teams and continued professional development should help. A greater danger lies in the undesirable formation of tracks. Because the pre-kindergarten program has a high percentage of students from low socioeconomic backgrounds, the make-up of the pre-K/K classes is inherently different than the K/1 classes. Bilingual program requirements cause similar problems. These realities, combined with prescriptive placement of weak readers in the early primary, has resulted in a disproportionate number of "high needs" kids in some classes. While we originally aimed for multi-age, multi-

> **Timeline for Student-Led Conferences**
>
> **March 7 - 11**
> Teachers receive planning packets
>
> **March 11 - 23**
> Parents receive invitations and time assignments
>
> **March 21**
> Faculty Meeting: Tips about 3-way conferences, primary and intermediate
>
> **March 23**
> 3-way conferences can begin
>
> **March 29**
> Release Day for 3-way conferences
>
> **After the conference**
> Teachers copy conference reports and place in white envelope in student folder

ethnic, and truly heterogeneous class populations, this hasn't worked out in every case, and remains a challenge to us all.

Meanwhile we are convinced that our move to multi-age classes was the best for us, our students, and their parents. We would never go back to the isolated, graded classrooms in which we spent all but the last four years of our teaching! Positive reactions from visitors to our program, convinces us we are right in our thinking. As a Mentor School for the State of Texas, we receive monthly visits throughout the year. Last year, 1,000 teachers, administrators, and parents visited Travis Heights. One of the most typical and telling comments they make is, "The children seem so relaxed and happy!" One administrator, after observing dismissal time, noted that rather than racing out of the building after hearing the bell ring, the children gather with their parents, teachers, and classmates, enjoying parting conversations, sometimes taking down an occasional note or giving a hug. This community building and teacher teaming makes multi-age more than worth the time and effort. ◆

What Do We Want Our Students To Know?

At Travis Heights successful students...

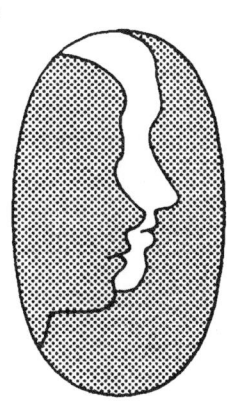

are contributing members of the global community

are technology literate

explore and appreciate the fine arts

make responsible choices

are involved in their own learning process

are life-long learners

are creative problem solvers

are team players

are able to set goals and work toward them

are able to communicate effectively

are healthy and have a positive self-image

perform academically at a quality level

These outcomes have been developed and revised annually over the past four years by students, teachers, and parents.

Multi-Age Reproducible 4.2

What Guides Instruction at Travis Heights?

District Scope and Sequence: a plan for each content area, i.e., math, language arts, social studies, science, that states what the district expects each student to learn.

National Content Area Standards: national standards for each subject area that are currently being defined by well-informed committees at the national level.

Teacher Expertise: the human touch - the knowledge of timing and pacing of learning processes, the ability to select topics that provide meaningful context for curricular content and allow the student to explore "big ideas" and make connections between various disciplines. Beyond this, students connect with the real world by sharing an individual teacher's area of special knowledge and high interest.

Current Events: real-world context that lends value to the content and skills required in the curriculum; an authentic and rich source that fosters high student *and* teacher interest.

Essential Elements: those concepts and skills identified by the State of Texas in each subject area that are considered as *essential* for every student to know.

TAAS specifications: an outline of specific objectives for each area tested; objectives serve as an instructional guide in meeting state requirements. [TAAS = Texas Assessment of Academic Skills]

NAPT specifications: information about the concepts that will be tested. [NAPT = Norm-referenced Assessment Program for Texas]

Textbook resources: a collection of content for various subject areas at various levels; supports the district plan.

Student Interest: the key to intrinsic motivation and a life-long learner mentality - learning that is student-initiated, thought-provoking, allows students to construct meaning, centers around real-world problems, and is open-ended to accommodate multiple learning styles and rates.

Benchmarks for Student Achievement

A comprehensive summary of what a student should be able to do...

by the end of 2nd grade

examples:

- Students can write simple paragraphs with a topic sentence and three to five sentences that support the main idea.

- Students can write a friendly letter, invitation and thank-you letters, and address the accompanying envelopes.

- Students can write a composition with a specific emphasis: descriptive and narrative.

by the end of 4th grade

examples:

- Students can write a three-paragraph composition.

- Students can write compositions for different purposes: to inform, to describe, to persuade, to tell a story.

Multi-Age Reproducible 4.4

Before the 3-Way Conference

Be sure portfolios are in order and ready.

In addition to using portfolio checklists, students should ask themselves, and each other, what they are most proud of; which selections show growth in their work; how they could edit a particular piece to make it better, more interesting or different; how they have organized their portfolios and why; etc. This kind of discussion should not just happen a day or two before the conference, of course, but throughout the year.

Model conference for students

Although it might reduce tensions connected with the conference to actually model or role play what a conference might look like, teachers and students can model *elements* of a good conference *all year long*. Reflecting on what one has heard, for example, is routine in classes that do "quick writes" following a whole-group reading selection. Teachers can reflect "out loud" by sharing with the class how they would change an activity to make it go more smoothly the next time. Some classes do a "week in review" response form to recap highlights, challenges, and new interests. Others produce student newsletters that go home to parents, or student-written individual letters to parents about a particular activity or topic.

Practice with students

Not only can mini-portfolio reviews occur between student and teacher, students can share their portfolios with peers and big or little buddies. Whole-group time can also be used to share selected items and get constructive feedback. Again, this should be an ongoing activity.

Be prepared to use open-ended questions and help students verbalize during conference

If open-ended questions are a habit in the classroom, students will more than likely have little trouble verbalizing. Good starters for a conference might be, "Tell me about how your portfolio is organized," or "Where did you get the idea to write this?"

Parent Invitation to 3-Way Conference

Dear Parent(s):

This is what you can expect when you attend the three-way parent(s) / teacher / child conference on
_____ at _____

You and your child will have time to look over his or her collection of work and the classroom displays and learning centers.

You and your child will then meet with me to discuss your child's strengths and any concerns, as well as set new learning goals for the upcoming term.

Your child is prepared to take an active part. There will be opportunities for you to ask questions, make comments, or express concerns.

Refreshments will be available in the library for your enjoyment following the conference on _____.
Baby-sitting for siblings will be provided during your conference time in the gym on that date as well.

If you have any issues you wish to discuss privately with me following the three-way conference, a sign-up sheet is available on the table by the door.

We believe that a three-way conference is one important way to support student learning. We look forward to meeting with you.

Sincerely,

Please return to your child's teacher tomorrow. Thank you.

Reader Reflections

Insights: _____

_____

_____

_____

_____

Actions for Our School (District) to Consider: _____

_____

_____

_____

_____

_____

_____

We are convinced our move to multi-age classes was the best for us. We would never go back to isolated, graded classrooms.

Debra Hime and Carolyn Moore
Travis Heights Elementary School

TEAMING FOR SUCCESS

How multi-age classrooms led to team teaching at two elementary schools, putting an end to classroom isolation.

5

Nine-year-old Jonathan and seven-year-old Delonte sat together on the rug sharing the picture book, *Possum Magic* by Mem Fox. They were practicing reading with expression, in preparation for reading the book to a kindergarten class the next day. As Jonathan finished his passage with great zest, I could hear Delonte say quietly to himself, "I need to read this good." And then he read with fluency and expression. He read phrases and paid attention to punctuation. His reading skill grew, his confidence grew, his social skills grew. Jonathan had been his model, his teacher. I smiled and thought, "And people wonder what is so glorious about teaching in a multi-age classroom." The tiny moments like that are glorious—children learning with peers in the same natural social setting they live in outside of school where interaction with kids of other ages is the norm.

Teachers Spur Change

I have had the joy of being a part of multi-age teaching and learning for the past nine years and I am sold. Not just for the growth I've seen in children like Delonte, but for the growth I've seen in teachers.

In my school system in Alexandria, Virginia, multi-age teaching has become a platform for restructuring. Teachers

KRIS CLARK
Lead Teacher
Mount Vernon Elementary School
Alexandria, Virginia

have used multi-age as a stepping stone to restructuring curriculum, assessment, grouping policies, and most important, teacher interaction and collegiality. Multi-age teaching and learning in my school system is a powerful reform tool. And in my district, the reform has been generated solely by teachers—not administrators or central office personnel. We teachers have looked hard at how we deliver instruction to our students. We have talked and read and researched. We have visited other schools and participated in staff development. And we have dreamed of ideal teaching situations for our students and for ourselves.

I teach at two kindergarten schools in the Alexandria school system. I am a lead teacher at Mount Vernon Elementary School. I am also a teacher at Cora Kelly Magnet school.

When asked what he was learning in kindergarten, Alex announced, "I'm in multi-age and I'm learning about oceans and books and how to work with my friends."

In both my schools, teachers dreamed of moving away from instructing in isolated, single-grade classrooms. Their reasons were sound. Children put together because they are close in chronological age, still have academic, social, and emotional needs that span several years. Those needs can best be met through a curriculum that allows students to approach tasks at their own developmental level. Teachers wanted academically successful students to have opportunities to excel and to learn at their own pace. They wanted to meet the needs of students who were at risk. Teachers wanted to spend more than one academic year with a group of students. And they wanted to teach in teams to share their knowledge and strengths. Overall, they wanted to offer students a richer, more complex curriculum. Teaming in multi-age classrooms became their solution.

Looking Back

My journey into multi-age teaching began many years ago when basals were in, writing meant copying off the blackboard, and most classrooms still had desks in a row. In 1985 I was teaching kindergarten at Cora Kelly Magnet School in Alexandria, Virginia. Alexandria is a city of 105,000 people across the river from Washington, D.C. Our student population was predominately minority with a shrinking middle-class enrollment. I taught at the only magnet school in the city. Cora Kelly was an inter-city school that had been converted to a neighborhood school with a magnet component. The school district hoped to attract nonminority students to racially balance the school. The magnet emphasis was science and technology. In its third year as a magnet, however, Cora Kelly still was not attracting enough nonminority students. I suggested to the school board that the only way to attract students from outside the neighborhood was to offer the best early childhood program in the city. They agreed and charged me with developing such a program.

That same spring I heard Barbara Day of the University of North Carolina speak at a conference. She spoke about Sewell Elementary School, a public school with multi-age classrooms. Her slides showed happy, engaged students working in learning centers with peers. The multi-age classrooms spanned two years, with two teachers and often two assistants. It didn't look or sound like the combination classes I remembered from my own youth, where the teacher tried to deliver separate curriculums to several grades. I was intrigued and wanted to know more. I began to think about teaming and asked Karen Mitsoff, a kindergarten colleague from another school who shared a similar philosophy and work ethic, if she was interested in developing a multi-age classroom. She was and our journey began.

Visits to Multi-Age Models

Karen and I traveled to Sewell Elementary School to see for ourselves how multi-age and team teaching worked. We had a notebook of questions. We spent two days in a classroom with students who worked independently and cooperatively. Students used learning contracts. They managed their time and were self-motivated. We were sold, but had more questions than answers. We returned to Sewell in September to see just how two teachers, Markie Prinkle and Kay Drake, began the school year developing such independent learners. Our September visit to Sewell answered more questions and convinced us that a two-year multi-age program offered teachers and students optimum opportunities for growth and development. On the plane ride home, we wrote our goals for the next year. Our goals included: developing a two-year, child-centered program organized around units of study; attracting nonminority students to the program; developing a high level of parent volunteerism; and creating strong achievement results for our students.

We returned home and convinced our school board that we needed time to develop an integrated curriculum for an effective multi-age pro-

Multi-Age Success Is Not a Fluke

Was our multi-age success at Cora Kelly Elementary a fluke or a viable organizational structure with a proven track record in regard to student achievement? Barbara Pavan's (*Nongradedness: Helping It To Happen*, 1993) research on the multi-age classroom was very encouraging and confirmed that our success was no fluke. Pavan compiled the results of sixty-four studies conducted between 1968 and 1990 on multi-age classrooms. Pavan's research gave the following conclusions:

1. Research studies comparing nongraded (multi-age) and graded schools provide a consistent pattern favoring nongradedness.

2. The nongraded groups performed better (58%) or as well (33%) as graded groups on measures of academic achievement.

3. On school attitudes, 52% of the studies indicated nongraded schools as better for students, 43% similar. Only 5% showed nongraded worse than graded schools.

4. The benefits to students of nongradedness increase as students have longer nongraded experiences.

5. African-American students, boys, students from low socioeconomic backgrounds, and underachievers benefit from a nongraded program.

gram. They agreed to pay us, and we agreed to write the curriculum and publicize the proposed multi-age program at preschools the spring before we began. The board also agreed to hire contractors to tear down the wall between our two classrooms, and build lofts to accommodate the learning centers we needed. Central Office secured grant money to outfit the classroom. It was an almost ideal situation—our idea, funded by grant money, with time to prepare. It isn't usually like that.

This change has occurred without mandates or directives from our Central Office.

Curriculum and Classroom Set Up

Karen and I spent two summers writing units of study that met the objectives and learning standards of our state and district. We wrote and collected materials for eighteen units—a two-year cycle. We alternated the units between a science focus (i.e., space, insects, weather) and a social studies focus (community, Native Americans, Chinese New Year).

In the Spring of 1988, we spoke to preschool parents across the city about the program and the benefits of a multi-age classroom. We prepared a slide show that illustrated developmentally appropriate teaching practices and integrated curriculum. We met with contractors to discuss removal of the wall between the two classrooms, and building lofts to house the learning centers. We ordered furniture and supplies. We continued to attend conferences on hands-on mathematics, whole-language strategies, and integrated curriculum ideas.

Learning Centers For Thematic Teaching

By July, enough children had been enrolled in our multi-age class to fill up every available seat. Our room was organized into two homebases and nine learning centers. The class was made up of twenty kindergartners and twenty first graders. Karen had a homebase of ten kindergartners and ten first graders. I had the same. Our homebases were heterogeneously mixed, and racially and sexually balanced. The goal of integration had been achieved in our classroom. The homebases were where the children congregated in the morning to organize for the day. Stories were read and shared. Directed lessons occurred there. The rest of the room was organized into learning centers—language arts, math, puzzles, housekeeping, blocks (unit and hollow), manipulatives, art, computers, and discovery. The discovery center carried the thematic unit we were studying at the time. We developed a weekly learning contract that helped students and teachers organize their day and week. The contract ensured that all children went to all centers in a given week. As students finished an activity in a particular center, they filled in the bubble on their contract and wrote a sentence about what they had done in the center.

The contracts allowed teachers to monitor a student's use of time and guide the student if necessary. The use of the contract allowed the children to make a plan for the day and for the week. It also encouraged independence and responsibility—two behaviors we wanted to foster.

Learning center activities were changed when all children had completed the activities. During learning center time, a teacher or assistant staffed the art center, the discovery center, the language arts center, and the math center. Often the centers reflected the unit of study. For example, the blocks center became a space shuttle and mission control during a space travel unit, while the art center was used to create amazing satellites from authentic materials. Academic centers had several levels of work and students completed tasks at their own pace. We did not distinguish between kindergarten work or first grade work, because some five-year-olds could do more advanced work than some seven-year-olds. The beauty of the program was the ease with which we could meet each child's needs.

Enlisting Parent Volunteers

In August of that year, we conducted home visits and began signing up parents to volunteer in class. Many of our minority parents did not have positive school experiences of their own and were uncomfortable in a school setting. By going to their homes, we illustrated a different level of caring than they remembered. We said, "We are advocates together for your child. We will work with you in any way we can. Please come to school and help us, even if it's only to cut out letters." Nearly all came and at conference time participation was 100 percent. Home visits sent a strong message and gained parent support and participation. In September we had a Parent Coffee to talk about parent concerns and expectations about volunteering. Parents volunteered for the amount of time they could afford. Those parents who could not come to school offered to work at home.

I knew we were on the right track when, later that Fall, a parent came to me with a story. Her family had gone to dinner with friends who had a daughter the same age as Alex, a five-year-old in our program. The dinner conversation turned to the children and what they were learning in kindergarten. The friend's daughter answered that she was learning "colors, letters, and sounds." When Alex was asked

Ingredients for a Successful Multi-Age Program

1. Visit sites that have a program similar to the one you're interested in starting.
2. Form a group of like-minded colleagues to support the effort.
3. Read everything you can about similar programs.
4. Prioritize goals.
5. Secure support from your school administration.
6. Allow time for writing curriculum, preferably in the summer when you're rested.
7. Share and borrow curriculum from other teachers.
8. Team teach with a partner who shares your philosophy and work ethic.
9. Ask for help from curriculum specialists, lead teachers, and community resources.
10. Be articulate and knowledgeable about why you are pursuing such a program.
11. Keep parents informed. They can be your strongest ally.

what he was learning, he announced, "I'm not in kindergarten, I'm in multi-age and I'm learning about oceans and books and how to work with my friends."

Two-Year Cycling

Seven years later, our K-1 multi-age classroom is thriving. There are long waiting lists to get into the program from minority and nonminority families. Each year half the class goes on to second grade and half stays. So each year Karen and I start the year with twenty seasoned students and ten new students each. Building a relationship with children and families over a two-year period is joyful and offers opportunities to bond, something not usually possible in a mere ten months.

The rewards are tremendous. My assistant, Peggy Pama, said to me one day, "You know, Kris, I've never worked so hard or had so much fun in all my years of teaching." Me either. As our success has become known, teachers and administrators from other school districts have begun to visit us. This has forced us to articulate, "Why are we doing what we are doing?" That question has become the benchmark for all of our decisions—"Is this good for the children, the parents, the teachers?" Resoundingly, the answer is yes. Children are happy learners, test scores of our students have been among the highest in the city, and parents are participating and engaging in their child's learning.

Benefits of Team Teaching

We teach with our doors open and have tried not to force our approach on colleagues. But slowly teachers have begun to borrow our units of study and we now plan culminating activities with other teachers. Even "traditional teachers" have started to set up learning centers. Desks have given way to tables so children can work together. When we run out of money for tables, we push desks together to support cooperative learning activities and centers. This change has occurred without mandates or directives from our central office. Our principal, Betty Hobbs, supports our changes and encourages team planning and interdisciplinary study.

During my work in multi-age classrooms at Cora Kelly, I also became a lead teacher for Mount Vernon Elementary School. Mount Vernon is strictly a neighborhood school with a large at-risk population. Seventy percent of our students receive free or reduced-price lunch. Many are non-English speaking. Mount Vernon is the largest elementary school in the district with close to 700 students in kindergarten through fifth grade. When I got to Mount Vernon, the test scores were the lowest in the city.

In my job as lead

To teach side by side with a colleague who shares a common vision and philosophy is a rich experience.

teacher, I served as staff developer, teaching coach, curriculum writer, and assessment developer. I was also in charge of improving instruction. Even with my strong commitment to multi-age, I knew better than to force it on teachers at Mount Vernon.

But powerful team teaching and student learning was occurring at Cora Kelly as a result of our multi-age efforts. To teach side by side with a colleague who shares a common vision and philosophy is a rich experience. Not only had Karen and I supported each other's teaching, but we had engaged in problem solving, cooperative planning, and collegial interaction for our students and our peers. Other teachers at Cora Kelly had caught the "team teaching bug" and were beginning to work together on integrated curriculum units. Karita Evans and Gigi Moon, for example, had taught next door to each other for ten years. They would plan lessons on the phone on Sunday evenings. When Karita lamented to me that she didn't want to let her first graders go at the end of the year, because she was enjoying their tremendous growth in writing, my reply was "Don't let them go. Keep them for second grade. Team with Gigi. After all, you've been planning together for years, why not share a room and children." She liked the idea. So did Gigi and our principal. Both decided to keep half of their first graders as second graders and take on twenty new first graders. Cora Kelly's principal, Betty Hobbs, promised to find the money to tear down the wall between their classrooms and recarpet. Karita and Gigi got busy writing units and developing plans for the next year. They leaned heavily on second grade teachers who had been developing units and team teaching for several years. They are now in their second year of multi-age teaching and love it. Their students are thriving and both teachers get to celebrate the growth and successes of their students over a two-year period. Cora Kelly now has four new multi-age classrooms. Fourth and fifth grade teachers have teamed up to offer four 4-5 grade classrooms. They chose teaching partners, rewrote their science and social studies curriculum to cover the objectives of both grade levels, opened up walls, organized centers and prepared for an exciting two-year cycle of learning.

Lonely Teachers Working in Isolation

When I went to Mount Vernon Elementary School, the differences were readily apparent. As the new lead teacher, I spent hours in other teachers' classrooms, working with students, modeling lessons, and coaching. What I discovered were lonely teachers, working in isolation, without the collegial in-

Our multi-age classroom and teaming led us to rethink our school, our instructional day, and our professional relationships.

teraction that I and other teachers at Cora Kelly had become used to in our multi-age classrooms. I knew the multi-age structure could offer teachers opportunities to end their classroom isolation.

My push toward teaming and multi-age teaching soon took hold. Teachers began to ask questions and investigate their options. I arranged for interested teachers to spend the day at a school in Fairfax County that had restructured for multi-age

Desks have given way to tables so children can work together.

teaching.

Mount Vernon's principal, Jalna Jones, supported the teachers' interest in multi-age and sent out a questionnaire asking teachers to dream of ideal teaching situations for the 1993-1994 school year. Did they want to teach in single grade, multi-age, or teams? She respected each teacher's personal journey toward change. No one was forced to teach in a team, and teachers that chose team teaching were allowed to pick their partners.

In the Fall of 1993, Mount Vernon began its journey into teaming and multi-age. We offered a K-1, 1-2, 2-3, and a 3-4 class. Two pairs of teachers chose to team, but in single-grade classrooms, so we also had a team teaching first grade together and a team teaching second grade together. All classes were heterogenously mixed by ability. We were careful to keep the mix of each classroom broad and diverse. The Mount Vernon teachers depended heavily on curriculum developed by Cora Kelly teachers, and on units of study they had developed themselves. We brainstormed common themes that reached across grade levels, and pulled material together. In the multi-age classes we concentrated on the curriculum guidelines for the older end of each class. Teachers in the 2–3 class taught third grade topics the first year and second grade topics the second year. This ensured that the third graders got both years of curriculum and not two years of second grade topics.

As classes began, I polled teachers on their anxiety level. My questions were, "What are you most worried about this year? What are you uncomfortable about?" Teachers were unanimously concerned about assessment. Every multi-age teacher felt a strong need to develop a more user-friendly assessment instrument, especially in language arts. With multi-age teachers fully embracing whole language and diverse reading and writing levels, the basal tests of the past did not meet our needs. I began collecting checklists and reading and writing records. We met regularly and pored over sample assessments. We eventually designed our own reading and writing curriculum.

But something even more important than assessment was happening in those meetings. We teachers shared belief systems, and philosophies. We discussed teaching strategies that worked and didn't work. We talked to each other about common concerns and celebrated progress and successes. This group of teachers that had ventured into teaming and multi-age teaching had become a support group of collegial problem solvers. We didn't meet because we were told to. We met because we wanted to. We had ideas to talk about and issues to discuss. We spent a relaxed weekend together at the beach talking about curriculum. We read professional books and discussed them. Our multi-age classrooms and teaming led us to rethink our school, our instructional day, and our professional relationships.

The Journey Continues

We are now in our second year of multi-age teaching at Mount Vernon. The teachers who teamed in single grades last year chose multi-age classes this year. One multi-age teacher, in her second year with the same class, says, "September was the smoothest beginning ever. So many students knew just what to do and what the expectations were. So many were such a big help with the younger students."

Several teachers invited their returning students to school for a picnic lunch the week before school began. They spent an hour remembering the beginning of school the previous year. They brainstormed how best to help the new students. Students recalled their own hesitancies. They talked about the meaning of friendship and cooperation. Those students returned on the first day of school ready to help, ready to model school behavior, ready to teach and learn.

Our multi-age journey continues. Our tasks are many. We are still rewriting assessment for language arts. We continue to create more interdisciplinary units of study. We continue to educate parents and administrators on the importance of not separating multi-age classes for assemblies, special programs, etc. We are trying to move toward terms like "multi-age primary" instead of "K–1." Our central office still insists that teachers be categorized as teaching first, second, third, etc. Their computers can't read "multi-age" yet. Our test results have improved, but still need attention. But for the multi-age teachers at Cora Kelly and Mount Vernon, the new classroom structures have been the impetus for rewriting curriculum, redesigning assessment, enhancing parent volunteerism, untracking students, and discovering the power and comfort of collegial support. As one teacher said to me, "We are building communities of learners, with children and teachers reading and writing and working together, supporting one another. This is how school should be for everyone." ◆

Multi-Age Reproducible 5.1

Student Learning Center Contract

Students must visit each of these Learning Centers during the week. As students finish an activity in a particular center, they fill in a circle on the contract and write a sentence about what they've done in the center.

Name _____ Week of _____

Language Arts
○ _____
○ _____

Math
○ _____
○ _____

Art
○ _____
○ _____

Discovery
○ _____
○ _____

Playhouse
○ ○

Listening
○ ○

Blocks
○ ○

Puzzles
○ ○

Manipulatives
○ ○

Home Base
○ ○

Computer
○ ○

Sand or Water
○ ○

Reader Reflections

Insights: _____

_____

_____

_____

_____

_____

Actions for Our School (District) to Consider: _____

_____

_____

_____

_____

_____

_____

_____

MULTI-AGE FROM THE GROUND UP

Scottsdale, Arizona, built its newest elementary school on a foundation of multi-age teaching and integrated thematic instruction.

6

In June 1993 we faced the most difficult challenge of our teaching careers.

Scottsdale, Arizona, had just opened it's newest school Aztec Elementary. Aztec was new in every sense of the word. A planning team of administrators, teachers, and parents decided an integrated curriculum would be essential to student learning. The team selected Susan Kovalik's Integrated Thematic Instruction Model (ITI) as the foundation of the new school. What's more, the team decided Aztec's 850 students would be placed in multi-age classrooms. Kovalik and other researchers recommend multi-age groupings because it puts kids in settings that mimic real life. As part of the new multi-age program, students would "loop" or "cycle" with a teacher for two years. We had several choices in regard to cycling. We teachers could choose to continue to the next level with our whole class, or we could send the older students on and receive a new set of younger students. Parents or teachers could decide to change student placement after the first year in the looping cycle. In some cases a student could stay with a teacher for three years.

Almost no one at our new school had experience teaching in a multi-age setting. We found ourselves grappling with the "how cans?" and the "what ifs?" We asked ourselves: how can we plan lessons appropriate for different ages? How can we convince parents that multi-age classes will benefit their children? What if the ability spread is too great for us to handle? What if the different ages don't get along? What if this doesn't work?

We knew, however, that August and opening day was fast approaching. We had to dig in our heels and just jump in.

BOBBIE FAULKNER
Teacher, grades 5-6
PATRICIA FAIVELEY
Teacher, grades 4-6

Aztec Elementary School
Scottsdale, Arizona

Research and Teacher Training

We began staff development in earnest with a series of workshops scheduled throughout the summer. We received training in how to implement Kovalik's ITI model. We also began pouring over research in regard to multi-age classrooms. Kovalik cites numerous benefits of multi-age groupings in her work. We reviewed research detailing how two-year cycles benefit both students and teachers. By

Intellectually we knew our stuff, but in reality we were worried.

the time school opened in August we had mixed feelings. Intellectually, we knew our stuff; but in reality we were worried.

We have encountered problems as we've built our multi-age program at Aztec. But the rewards we've reaped by meeting the challenges head on more than make up for the frustrations. We have never worked harder, but we have never enjoyed our classes more. Our success is based on a number of factors. We employ a variety of cognitive learning styles to guide us in our teaching. Our students are arranged in Learning Clubs for greater cooperative learning. And we have a strong education and outreach program to enlist parent support for multi-age classes.

Strategies For Multi-Age Implementation

Our multi-age program is built around particular themes and learning theories that give us focus and remind us of our goals.

Integrated Thematic Instruction (ITI)

At Aztec Elementary, instruction is student driven, and integrates a number of themes. Real life is integrated and we know that school should mimic the real world as closely as possible. Social studies or science-related, year-long themes that are age-appropriate and real-world related, work best. The year-long theme is at the heart of the Aztec classroom. Some themes we've used include: habitats, the environment, and ecological systems. Each theme is divided into several components. For example, a theme on Stones and Bones is divided into lesson plans on the Stone Age, becoming civilized, bats, caves, and archaeology. Our integrated curriculum allows teachers to stop being the "sage on the stage" and become the "guide on the side."

Creative Scheduling

We use several scheduling innovations to minimize fragmentation, which can be disastrous in multi-age programs. The goal is to reduce the number of pullout periods or times during the day when students are required to go to other classrooms for instruction. We use a twelve-day schedule to accommodate special subjects, allow time for planning, and provide blocks of learning time. Pullouts are limited to fitness and music only. Art is taught in the classroom for ninety minutes. We also lengthened lunch periods to an hour. This gives ample time for band and orchestra rehearsals. There are no pullouts for students with special needs; instead the resource teacher comes to the classroom, integrating help into the regular program. This schedule produces minimum disruption and optimum learning time.

Life Skills and Lifelong Guidelines

Life Skills and Lifelong Guidelines (see Reproducibles 6.2 and 6.3 a & b) are an integral part of Susan Kovalik's ITI model. The guidelines are based on brain research. The guidelines encourage students to respect themselves and others. When followed consistently, the guidelines guarantee that students can remain in a learning mode, rather than operating from an emotional base. The Life Skills provide parameters that help students evaluate their own performance. Students are guided—individually and in groups—to an understanding of social behaviors that enhance their success.

At Aztec we live and breathe the Life Skills and Lifelong Guidelines. They have become our discipline plan. The guidelines appear all over campus—in our morning announcements, on our monitors, and in the cafeteria. Everyone from custodians to fitness instructors use the guidelines every day. We even integrate Life Skills into literature lessons.

Limited Class Size

Maximum class size at Aztec Elementary is twenty-five students. Many of us teachers have come from schools where classes of thirty students or more are the norm. Our principal, Hulk Fitter, achieved the class size standard using what we call "creative financing." In a major money-saving move, Aztec hired classified personnel for some positions previously reserved for certified teachers. This provided funds for additional classroom teachers and thus reduced class size. Our Instructional Resource Facilitators are highly qualified in their fields. They just don't hold teaching degrees. Instructional facili-

Welcome to Aztec

Scottsdale Unified School District is dedicated to the principle of integrated instruction and lifelong learning. The district outcomes reflect this commitment to innovative instruction throughout the K-12 district. Scottsdale Unified school district has 16 elementary schools, 4 junior high, and 3 high schools, with the fourth scheduled to open Fall of 1995.

Opened in 1993, Aztec Elementary is the first school in the district to totally implement integrated thematic instruction in a brain-compatible, multi-aged environment. The population at Aztec Elementary is comprised mostly of professional families with post-high school education levels. It is located in the fastest growing area of North Scottsdale, with a current enrollment of 850 students. Enrollment is projected at 925 for the 1995-96 school year. Enrollment will level out to 850 K - 5 students after the sixth graders leave for a new junior high school expected to open in 1996.

Aztec is continuously visited by professionals from across the country and parents who are interested in how a multi-age school works. In 1993-94 we had over 900 visitors at Aztec. Aztec has established, in a short 18 months, a reputation for being a school of excellence. The school has become a model for others wishing to implement multi-age. We are in the process of becoming a lab school for student teachers in conjunction with Grand Canyon University of Phoenix. We believe in the old African proverb: "It takes an entire village to raise a child."

tators provide instruction in art, technology, media services, and fitness. They are an integral part of our staff and everyone considers them teachers in every sense of the word. This substitution is somewhat controversial in some circles, but has served our staff and student body well.

Project Based Activities
Our student's school days are filled with projects and hands-on activities that incorporate a variety of skills. These activities allow the student to be an active participant, rather than a passive spectator. We believe that projects can showcase real learning better than a constant barrage of fill in the blank ditto sheets. We have a saying: "Dittos don't build dendrites."

Cooperative Learning
We know that by working in groups, students learn from each other and learn to work together. This useful technique works for all classrooms, but is particularly effective in multi-age settings.

Multiple Intelligences
All Aztec teachers plan lessons and projects using the multiple intelligences theory as outlined by Howard Gardner and David Lazear. This approach allows students to fully use their learning strengths. Using the multiple intelligences model provides opportunity for students to function at their individual level. Students can reach within and bring out their personal best.

Brain Compatible Learning Environment
Learning environments must be structured so that students can remain "up shifted" and learning can take place. Kovalik outlines eight brain-compatible components designed to promote learning and we work to implement them all (see Reproducible 6.5).

Flexible Student Grouping
At Aztec we have eliminated ability grouping, tracking, and departmentalization. We organize students into groups by interest, at random, or short-term for skill enhancement. Our groupings are flexible and temporary.

Authentic Assessment
We use a variety of authentic assessments to measure student academic growth. The major forms we use include portfolios, performance tasks, products, and exhibition projects.

We make sure to write student evaluations using Bloom's Taxonomy, which outlines several levels of thinking and provides an easy and powerful vehicle for curriculum development (see Reproducible 6.6).

Curriculum and Teaching Methods
We use the above guidelines and learning theories to enhance our teaching and curriculum. We use a variety of teaching methods throughout our

We grappled with the "How cans?" and "what ifs?" However, we just simply had to jump in.

school. Many of our classrooms use learning centers or clubs. Learning clubs support our thematic lessons and are also used for skill development. For example, we had an entire learning club (five classrooms, ages 5-10) plant a garden and then develop learning centers focused on the garden activities. The garden was a monthly component of the club's year-long theme.

We develop students' writing skills through workshops and student journals. Writing is also integrated throughout the curriculum through letter writing, reports, publishing original works, and note taking.

Our classrooms are literature-based. Children read quality literature that is age appropriate and relevant to their experiences. Some of our colleagues use learning packets, contracts, and individualized programs to guide students in basic skills.

Projects are an integral part of the assessment process as well. We expect students to give presentations throughout the year, based on their own research in particular areas.

Benefits Of Multi-Age Classes

In our brief existence we have already begun to see the advantages that our teaching methods and learning theories provide. Aztec teachers were recently surveyed and listed the following as benefits of multi-age groupings:

Continuance: This was number one on everyone's list. Our teachers love spending two years with their class. Cycling or looping provides more time to teach a continuum of skill. Teachers become more familiar with students and don't have to worry about start-up time at the beginning of the second year. However, we firmly believe that in the second year both the teacher and the parent must have the right to request a different experience for the student.

Retention: Multi-age classes reduce the need for student retention. This benefit was most often cited by primary level teachers. A student who needs more time to master the continuum of skills and concepts can spend two years in a class without failing a grade or being held back. One teacher reminded us that age and development are not always on a parallel timetable. Students often need extra time to allow development to "catch-up."

Special Needs: Teachers feel that servicing special needs students is facilitated in a multi-age setting. Students can identify with a range of both social and academic levels. Overt forms of labeling are avoided.

Diversity: Our school population is not very ethnically or racially diverse. Our teachers be-

---

Laying the Foundation For Aztec

In 1992 Scottsdale, Arizona, school superintendent Dr. Duane Sheldon and the school governing board decided they wanted a school planned from its inception to provide the best learning environment for children. A school not tied to the way things had always been done. Throughout the year a strategic plan was hammered out by groups of parents, teachers, students, administrators, and community supporters. Arthur Anderson and Company, a consulting firm, was brought in to help facilitate the process, and formulate the best educational ideas for Aztec. The resulting Arthur Anderson study contained fourteen points for improved educational productivity. We are guided by these fourteen points in our work at Aztec Elementary School (see Reproducible 6.1).

lieve multi-age classrooms provide an important opportunity for our students to experience diversity. We feel that working with different age levels lead children to respect individual differences.

Pitfalls Along The Way

Opening a new school is always a challenge. Aztec experienced many of the usual glitches and bugs that occur when new systems are put into place. But because we implemented so many new ideas at once, our problems were multiplied. The multi-age concept in an educational setting was not familiar to our community, hence it generated the most confusion. Looking back, these were the major frustrations of our fledgling year.

Parental Misunderstandings

Anyone implementing multi-age classrooms should expect some controversy from parents. We didn't, and were shocked when we encountered it. We thought all parents would think multi-age was as wonderful as we did. The biggest snag we encountered during our first year, involved parent reaction to student age groupings. In the beginning we had six age divisions incorporating two grade levels each: ages 5-6 (grades K-1); ages 5-6-7 (grades 1-2); ages 6-7-8 (grades 2-3); ages 8-9-10 (grades 3-4); ages 9-10-11 (grades 4-5); and ages 10-11-12 (grades 5-6).

We thought further divisions would offer more flexibility and give every student the best possible learning placement. That did not turn out to be the case. There was too much overlap. With some ages, there were up to three possible placements. Some parents completely misunderstood the placement process. Furthermore, labeling the classes by ages, rather than the more customary grade levels confused the community.

The most prevalent complaint was voiced by parents who were afraid that if their child was among the eldest in a group, the child wouldn't be challenged. Some parents worried the curriculum might be "watered down" for younger students. This was especially true for the middle and upper levels. For example, if an eight-year-old child was placed in a 6-7-8 class instead of an 8-9-10 class, some parents felt the 6-7-8 was a lower placement. Even some teachers on the staff, whose children were attending Aztec, had to struggle to shift their thinking in this regard.

To a reasonable point, we tried to accommodate parents wishes to move their child "up." But quickly a trickle became an avalanche. It wasn't long before there were simply no spaces left in the classes parents were requesting. A few angry parents placed their children in another school, while others begrudgingly had no choice but to remain.

The total number of dissatisfied parents was

Our student days are filled with projects and hands-on activities that incorporate a variety of skills.

small, but vocal. Two sets of parents even went so far as to contact the local newspaper to air their grievances publicly. Both families had students in the 8-9-10 grouping and wanted them placed "up" in the 10-11-12 classes.

This negative publicity affected the morale of our faculty. However, the furor gradually died down. Most of the parents who retained their kids in Aztec discovered that not only was the situation not so bad, in many cases it was surprisingly wonderful! The horrors they dreaded simply did not materialize. The reality is, that in multi-age classrooms there are no "high" or "low" placements.

Over time we have developed a thicker skin to deal with controversy over our multi-age program. We have learned not to take every question or criticism so personally. As each year progresses and understanding of the multi-age concept increases, the controversy dies down considerably.

It is important to note, however, that there is less controversy when it is the parents choice to place a child in a multi-age class. If you are considering starting a multi-age program at your school, we suggest you do research, plan ahead, and get the support of your administrator. Then you should hold informational meetings with parents and explain your plans and goals.

Inadequate Time For Planning

Teachers unanimously agree that planning for multi-age classes is extremely time consuming. Planning must be thematic, conceptual, and skills-based. We do not rely on grade level textbooks and ditto sheets. Instead, we plan projects and activities that are age appropriate, brain compatible, and adaptable to multiple intelligences. Release time for team/age-level planning is essential, but not always easy to arrange.

Too Much Hype

Aztec Elementary School received a lot of positive attention from the media and the community before the school opened. Our planning team worked

---

Tips For Successful Multi-Age Teaching

- **Flexibility:** Change plans and adjust expectations as indicated by student progress. Keep your lesson plans flexible.
- **Integrated Thematic Instruction:** Base your instruction on a theme rather than a textbook. Incorporate skills with theme instruction.
- **Cooperative Learning:** Let children learn from and with each other. Pair a youngster at the early stage of acquiring a skill, with a student who is more confident but still needs practice. Work in cooperative groups.
- **Multiple Intelligences:** Get familiar with the multiple intelligence theories that have emerged from current brain research.
- **Brain Compatible Classrooms:** Setting up a brain compatible classroom following the model of Susan Kovalik, is a great help in a multi-age classroom
- **Bloom's Taxonomy:** Be aware of and teach higher-level thinking skills.
- **Authentic Assessment:** Use a variety of methods to assess your student progress.
- **Give Up Being "The Sage On The Stage" And Become "The Guide On The Side":** Let students have more say in the planning and implementation of their learning. Listen to what they already know.

hard to try to educate students and their families about our philosophy and innovative methods. Local newspapers touted Aztec as a panacea for the educational problems facing society. Later, we wondered if the publicity had worked against us. It is possible expectations were so high that they were virtually unattainable. Perhaps a lower-key "birth" would have been a better choice.

All of us plan lessons and projects using the multiple intelligences theory as outlined by Howard Gardner and David Lazear.

Paving Over Pitfalls

We employed a number of strategies to fix the conditions that had caused the major problems. Under the guidance of our principal and assistant principal—along with support from our Site-based Decision-Making Team—we put our heads together and came up with workable solutions. Here are the changes we made:

Streamline Class/Age Offerings: We streamlined our age offerings with several choices for the younger ages but fewer ones for the upper levels. Now our classes are identified by the more familiar grade names and follow a predictable pattern. In the 1995-96 school year the levels will be K; K-1; 1-2; 3-4; 5-6. This year (1994-95), one each of the 2-3 and 4-5 levels remained because those teachers wanted to continue with their classes from last year. But they will be eliminated in the future so the student can alternate between being the youngest and oldest in a group during each two-year cycle. In 1996, we will lose our sixth graders to a new middle school. Grades 4-5 will then be the oldest grouping.

Learning Clubs: Our faculty is organized into Learning Clubs. Small groups of teachers meet twice monthly to discuss topics of mutual concern and interest. Learning Clubs are encouraged to read and discuss research and curriculum themes. Our learning clubs are generally organized according to grade levels. But this is not a hard and fast rule. We do make sure, however, that Learning Clubs contain a mix of experienced and newer teachers. Learning Clubs provide a much-needed support system for teachers. Our Learning Clubs are operating better in this, our second year, than they did initially. Like many other things, practice makes perfect.

Theme Planning Time: There is never as much planning time as we want, but we have made considerable progress. We have increased our team planning time significantly. A parent is organizing a corps of volunteer parent substitutes. The parents will volunteer one-half day per month for teacher planning time. Our principal has also arranged for each teacher to have one-half day per grading period for team planning. Now an entire Learning Club can meet for theme planning. We are exploring additional options, but for now what we have is very helpful.

Parent Education: To educate and inform parents about our efforts we hold dozens of meetings in the community. Some meetings are held in private homes. At each meeting we give parents information on brain-compatible learning environments and multi-age teaching. Throughout our first year, we especially communicated with parents at open houses and parent conferences. We recognize the need for continuing education, especially for families new to the community.

Conclusion

This is Aztec's story. Every community is different and will react to changes in different ways. At Aztec, teachers, parents, and students are realizing the benefits of multi-age groupings. We believe in the old African proverb: "It takes an entire village to raise a child." That is what we have tried to do, work hand-in-hand with our community to provide the best educational experience possible.

Not everyone is fortunate enough to have the opportunity to start a new school like we did. Even when new schools are built, they are rarely planned from their inception to be as innovative as Aztec. We feel lucky to be able to work with like-minded professionals and an involved parent community. But even if your situation is different from ours, we encourage you to be the catalyst for change for the better in your district. MULTI-AGE is worth the battle. It's good for kids. GO GET IT!! ◆

Multi-Age Reproducible 6.1

Fourteen Points For Improved Educational Productivity

Consulting firm Arthur Anderson and Company, worked with Aztec parents, teachers, and administrators to formulate the best educational ideas for our new school. Following are the fourteen points developed for improved education quality:

1. Commit to first-time quality
2. Focus on each student as a customer
3. Increase student motivation
4. Align curriculum with strategic goals
5. Align teaching and testing with curricular objectives
6. Integrate curricular objectives
7. Utilize students as a resource
8. Increase student engagement
9. Focus technology on the classroom
10. Link schools and the home
11. Expand student learning time
12. Reduce nonproductive time
13. Introduce flexible scheduling
14. Transform teachers from lecturers to managers.

Lifelong Guidelines

Lifelong guidelines are an integral part of Susan Kovalik's ITI model. These guidelines are reinforced each day among students throughout our campus.

Trustworthiness
To act in a manner that makes one worthy of confidence.

Truthfulness
Telling the truth is about personal responsibility and mental accountability.

Active Listening
Listening with intention involves more than just hearing.

No Put-Downs
The classroom must become an island where students can be free from put-downs.

Personal Best
Personal best says it is not the teacher alone who determines success, but rather you are given guidelines to evaluate your own performance against the life skills.

Multi-Age Reproducible 6.3a

Life Skills

Integrity
To conduct oneself according to a sense of what's right and wrong.

Initiative
To do something because it needs to be done.

Flexibility
The ability to alter plans when necessary.

Perseverance
To continue in spite of difficulties.

Organization
To plan, arrange, and implement in an orderly way; to keep things in an orderly, readily usable way.

Sense of Humor
To laugh and be playful without hurting others.

Effort
To try your hardest.

Common Sense
To use good judgment.

Continued

Life Skills (continued)

Problem Solving
To seek solutions in difficult situations and everyday problems.

Responsiblity
To respond when appropriate, to be accountable for your actions.

Patience
To wait calmly for someone or something, sometimes over a long period of time.

Friendship
To make and keep a friend or friends through mutual trust and caring.

Curiosity
A desire to learn or know about one's world.

Cooperation
To work together toward a common goal or purpose.

Caring
To feel concern for others.

Courage
The ability to do what is right even if afraid.

Life Skills are also part of Susan Kovalik's ITI model and can be found throughout our campus.

Multi-Age Reproducible 6.4

And The Survey Says...

Here are some comments from a teacher survey on multi-age teaching at Aztec Elementary School:

"This type of grouping brings out a more cooperative, less competitive spirit, so the students help each other more. It teaches children to compete with themselves."
—Cathy Mooney

"Multi-age makes facilitating cooperative education so much easier. It also forces the teacher out of the control role into a facilitator role."
—Lucy Kastelic

"It is a lot of pressure to ensure students have met every skill at every level of understanding when curriculum expectations are still in place."
—Sarah Calvin

"Children learn to accept and respect differences. They realize that learning is a process."
—Mary Anne Duggan

"I love, love, love it!"

—Brenda Chadwick

Brain Compatible Learning

The learning environment must be structured so that students can remain "upshifted" into their cerebral cortex and learning can take place. Therefore, the learning environment must consciously promote the eight brain-compatible components. We are grateful to educator, author, and lecturer Susan Kovalik for teaching us about the following components, and their importance to the growth of our children and to us as lifelong learners:

1 Absence of Threat denotes the importance of creating a trustworthy environment where danger, real or perceived, is absent for the child. There are no put-downs and the dignity of all learners is promoted.

2 Meaningful Content is from real life, the natural world around us. It depends heavily upon prior experience, is age-appropriate and thus understandable. It is significant to the learner and is rich enough to allow for pattern-seeking as a means of identifying and creating meaning. It can be used within the life of the learner and does not involve an external reward system.

3 Choices provide the ultimate determiner of success. Choices permit the learner to build independence as a learner by providing ample opportunity to create and/or select learning processes and situations that are meaningful for the learner and, in so doing, builds confidence and competence.

4 Adequate Time is needed to get the job of learning done well, to accomplish mastery (the ability to use the concept/skill in real-life settings), to fully understand the connections among prior learnings and learning yet to come.

5 Enriched Environment provides the learner with firsthand sources, immersed in reality. Enriched environment provides broad-based resource materials. It is body-compatible, avoids distractions and overstimulation, stays current, and increases input at least ten times over what it is in traditional classrooms.

6 Collaboration means building strong and positive interpersonal relationships. A strong cornerstone for interpersonal relationships is essential. Children are afforded the opportunity to "work together" for the accomplishment of a common goal. This is not two or more students working together on the same assignment. True collaboration means there is a sense of group, built and maintained by attention to process and to the development of social skills.

7 Immediate Feedback is being selective in what you assess and utilizing the two basic tenets behind the authentic assessment movement: assess what is of value and make sure that the product or project utilized for assessing students is one that has worth to the student in and of itself.

8 Mastery is the goal of brain compatible learning. Personal best is emphasized and the learner understands a skill or concept and can apply it to real-life situations. Children don't have time to do it over and over. Teach to mastery the first time.

Multi-Age Reproducible 6.6

Bloom's Taxonomy of Cognitive Objectives

For 30 years, Benjamin Bloom's Taxonomy has provided an easy and powerful vehicle for curriculum development. Each level of thinking is followed by action words or process verbs to help you recognize what level of question you are asking.

Knowledge	The student recalls or recognizes information: define, repeat, list, memorize, name, label, record, recall, relate, tell, report, narrate.
Comprehension	The student changes information into a different symbolic form: restate, describe, explain, identify, report, discuss, recognize, express, locate, review.
Application	The student solves a problem using the knowledge and appropriate generalizations: demonstrate, practice, apply, interview, translate, dramatize, operate, schedule, illustrate, interpret.
Analysis	The student separates information into component parts: debate, distinguish, question, differentiate, solve, diagram, compare, inventory, criticize, experiment.
Evaluation	The student makes qualitative and quantitative judgments according to set standards: select, judge, predict, choose, estimate, measure, value, rate, assess.
Synthesis	The student solves a problem by putting information together that requires original, creative thinking: compose, propose, formulate, assemble, construct, design, arrange, organize, prepare, classify, plan.

Reader Reflections

Insights: _____

_____

_____

_____

_____

_____

Actions for Our School (District) to Consider: _____

_____

_____

_____

_____

_____

_____

_____

_____

Selected Resources

Books

Anderson, R. and Goodlad, J. 1987. *The Nongraded Elementary School*. New York: Teachers College Press.

Anderson, R. and Pavan, B.N. 1993. *Nongradedness: Helping It To Happen*. Pennsylvania: Technomic Publishing Co.

Azwell, T.S., Foyle, H.C., and Lyman, L. 1993. *Cooperative Learning in the Elementary Classroom*. Washington, D.C.: National Education Association.

Burns, R.C. 1993. *Parents and Schools: From Visitors to Partners*. Washington, D.C.: National Education Association.

Cangelosi, J.S. 1984. *Cooperation in the Classroom: Students and Teachers Together*. Washington, D.C.: National Education Association.

Chase, P. and Doan, J. 1994. *Full Circle: A New Look at Multiage Education*. New Hampshire: Heinemann.

Erb, T.O. and Doda, N.M. 1989. *Team Organization*. Washington, D.C.: National Education Association.

Feuerstein, R., Fischer, K.W., Knight, C.C., Presseisen, B.Z., and Sternberg, R.J. 1990. *Learning and Thinking Styles: Classroom Interaction*. Washington, D.C.: National Education Association.

Fogarty, R. 1993. *The Multiage Classroom: A Collection*. Illinois: Skylight Publishing.

Forte, I. and Schurr, S. 1993. *The Definitive Middle School Guide*. Nashville, Tenn.: Incentive Publications.

Gardner, H. 1983. *Frames of Mind, The Theory of Multiple Intelligences*. New York: Basic Books.

Grant, J. and Johnson, B. 1995. *A Common Sense Guide to Multi-Age Practices*. Teachers Publishing Group.

Gullo, D.F. 1992. *Developmentally Appropriate Teaching in Early Childhood*. Washington, D.C.: National Education Association.

Irvin, J.L. 1992. *Transforming Middle Level Education*. Mass.: Allyn and Bacon.

Lawler, D.S. 1991. *Parent-Teacher Conferencing in Early Childhood Education*. Washington, D.C.: National Education Association.

Lawlor, J.C., Neubert, G.A., and Stover, L.T. 1993. *Creating Interactive Environments in the Secondary School*. Washington, D.C.: National Education Association.

Lescher, M.L. 1995. *Portfolios: Assessing Learning in the Primary Grades.* Washington, D.C.: National Education Association.

Maeda, B. 1994. *The Multi-Age Classroom, A Look at One Community of Learners.* Creative Teaching Press.

Pattillo, J. and Vaughan, E. 1992. *Learning Centers for Child-Centered Classrooms.* Washington, D.C.: National Education Association.

Reiff, J.C. 1992. *Learning Styles.* Washington, D.C.: National Education Association.

Rottier, J., and Ogan, B.J. 1991. *Cooperative Learning in Middle-Level Schools.* Washington, D.C.: National Education Association.

Slavin, R.E. 1991. *Student Team Learning: A Practical Guide to Cooperative Learning.* Washington, D.C.: National Education Association.

Walmsley, S. A. 1994. *Children Exploring Their World: Theme Teaching in Elementary School.* New Hampshire: Heinemann.

Time Strategies. NEA Teacher-to-Teacher Books. 1994. Washington, D.C.: National Education Association.

Student Portfolios. NEA Teacher-to-Teacher Books. 1993. Washington, D.C.: National Education Association.

Articles, Papers, and Reports

Bozzone, M.A. 1995. "Straight Talk From Multi-Age Classrooms." *Instructor.*

Elkind, D. 1987. "Multi-Age Grouping." *Young Children.*

Gaustad, J. 1992. "Making the Transition from Graded to Nongraded Primary Education." *Oregon School Study Council Bulletin.*

Gullo, D. 1992. "Developmentally Appropriate Teaching in Early Childhood." National Education Association.

Gutierrez, R., and Slavin, R. 1992. "Achievement Effects of the Nongraded Elementary School: A Retrospective Review." Center for Research on Effective Schooling for Disadvantaged Students. Baltimore, Maryland.

Hunter, M. 1992. "How to Change to a Nongraded School." Association for Supervision and Curriculum Development (ASCD).

Katz, L. 1994. "Nongraded and Mixed-Age Grouping In Early Childhood Programs." ERIC Clearinghouse on Elementary and Early Childhood Education. Urbana, Illinois.

Katz, L.G., Evangelou, D., and Hartman, J.A. 1990. "The Case for Mixed-Age Grouping in Early Childhood."

Washington, D.C.: National Association for the Education of Young Children.

Marzano, R. 1992. "A Different Kind of Classroom." Association for Supervision and Curriculum Development (ASCD).

Sumner, D. 1993. "Multiage Classrooms: The Ungrading of America's Schools. The Multiage Resource Book." Society for Developmental Education. Peterborough, New Hampshire.

"Teaching and Learning in the Multigrade Classroom: Student Performance and Instructional Routines." ERIC Digest, ERIC Clearinghouse on Rural Education and Small Schools. Charleston, West Virginia. 1991

"The Nongraded Primary: Making Schools Fit Children." American Association of School Administration, Arlington, Virginia. 1992.

Videos

Mixed-Age Grouping at the Olive Mary Stitt School. 1993; VHS. United Learning, 6633 W. Howard Street., P.O. Box 48718, Niles, IL 60714-0718.

The Nongraded School. (30 minutes; VHS). Agency for Instructional Technology. Box A, 111 W. 17th Street, Bloomington, IN 47404-3019.

New Age Learning - Cross Age Tutoring. National Education Association and The Learning Channel. Teacher TV episode 8. Washington, D.C.: NEA Professional Library.

Teaching the Academically Diverse Classroom. National Education Association and The Learning Channel. Teacher TV episode 22. Washington, D.C.: NEA Professional Library.

Throwing Out Rigid Structures. National Education Association and The Learning Channel. Teacher TV episode 18. Washington, D.C.: NEA Professional Library.

Notes:

_____

_____

_____

_____

_____

_____

Personal Resources

Individuals:

Publications:

Personal Resources

_____   _____
_____   _____
_____   _____
_____   _____

Organizations: _____

_____   _____
_____   _____
_____   _____
_____   _____
_____   _____
_____   _____
_____   _____
_____   _____
_____   _____

Glossary

Assessment
Any systematic basis for making inferences about a student's learning progress.

Alternative Assessment
Any assessment form other than standardized tests, commercial tests, worksheets, or textbook questions.

Block Scheduling
Restructuring the school day into fewer, longer instructional time blocks.

Classroom Management
Arranging the classroom environment to produce successful student involvement and cooperation. This includes room arrangement, curriculum, instructional techniques, classroom rules, and expectations.

Climate
The shared perception of the way things are. In other words, the shared perceptions that those associated with a school have about the school's policies, practices, and procedures.

Collegiality
Collaborative teamwork that pulls together the best efforts of all concerned.

Continuous Progress
Children remain with their classroom peers regardless of whether they have met or surpassed pre-specified grade-level achievement expectations. The goal is to let each child progress at his or her individual rate of learning and development.

Cooperative Learning
Students work in small groups to help one another master academic material. Interaction can range from pairs discussing an anticipatory set of questions for five minutes, to trios working on complex multiday units.

Culture
The system of shared meanings, assumptions, and underlying values (or philosophy) of an organization.

Cycling
Students remain with the same teacher or teaching team for two or more years. Also referred to as "looping," or student-teacher progression.

Integrated Thematic Instruction
Combining academic subjects (social studies, science, history, language arts, etc.) to teach a particular theme or lesson plan.

Learning Centers
A defined space within a classroom where materials are organized in such a way that children learn without the teacher's constant presence and direction. In learning centers, children interact with materials and other students.

Multi-Age, Mixed-Age Grouping
Placing children together in classes without grade-level designations, and with more than a one-year age span. Typically, students have the same teacher (or teaching team) for two or three years. With the beginning of each new school year, only the older students enter new classes.

Multi-Grade, Mixed-Grade Grouping
Students of different ages taught in the same classroom. However, grade-level designations are maintained, along with separate curricula for students in each grade.

Multiple Intelligences
Learning theory put forth by Howard Gardner that states students can exhibit their intelligence in many different ways.

Nongraded or Ungraded Grouping
Similar to mixed- or multi-age grouping.

Outcome
Learning behavior or competency.

Portfolio
A record of learning that focuses on a student's work and often his or her reflections on that work. Material may be collected by the student, or in collaboration with teachers and parents.

Pullout Programs
Instructional activities such as speech therapy, music, or art, for which a student leaves the regular classroom on a short-term, scheduled basis.

Retention
When students are kept from progressing to the next grade level because they have not successfully completed work in their current grade.

Student-led Conferences
A form of assessment. Student leads the presentation of his or her portfolio before the teacher and parent.

Team Teaching
Two or more teachers join together to teach one group of students.

Notes:

_____

_____

_____

_____

_____

_____

The true philosophy of nongradedness is the belief that individuals are unique and need different treatments to reach their maximum growth potential.

Robert Anderson and
Barbara Nelson Pavan
<u>Nongradedness: Helping It To Happen</u>